THE LEADERSHIP BET

GREAT LEADERSHIP TRANSFORMS LIVES

BILL PARTIN

Copyright © 2020 Bill Partin.

All rights reserved. No part of this book may be reproduced, stored, or transmitted by any means—whether auditory, graphic, mechanical, or electronic—without written permission of the author, except in the case of brief excerpts used in critical articles and reviews. Unauthorized reproduction of any part of this work is illegal and is punishable by law.

This book is a work of non-fiction. Unless otherwise noted, the author and the publisher make no explicit guarantees as to the accuracy of the information contained in this book and in some cases, names of people and places have been altered to protect their privacy.

ISBN: 978-1-7165-6581-6 (sc)
ISBN: 978-1-7165-6579-3 (e)

Library of Congress Control Number: 2020918612

Because of the dynamic nature of the Internet, any web addresses or links contained in this book may have changed since publication and may no longer be valid. The views expressed in this work are solely those of the author and do not necessarily reflect the views of the publisher, and the publisher hereby disclaims any responsibility for them.

Lulu Publishing Services rev. date: 09/28/2020

DEDICATION

To Kim, my partner in life. Thank you for your never-ending support, your unconditional love and for being my Nathan, my Jonathan, and my Samuel.

To those dedicated to being a servant leader and providing great leadership to your team, please visit www.theleadershipbet.com and use the passcode Timetorock to view downloadable resources mentioned in this book.

ACKNOWLEDGEMENTS

I want to thank my wife Kim for being with me start to finish, and every step in between on this project. You're a rock star!

Thank you, Coach Pam, for encouraging me to write my story. Thank you, Mom and Dad, for planting in me a desire to work on getting better everyday and for helping me see the glass is always half full.

Thanks to my Dad/Gramps Support Team – Kari, Dylan, Jaxon, Kazen, Kyle, Julie, CC, and Claire for letting me share this crazy idea of writing a book and for keeping a straight face! You all are loved and appreciated each day!

Thanks to my Book Team – Hailey, Travis, Chad, Dizzy, Kim, and Coach Pam for reading the early drafts, listening to the ideas, and encouraging me along the way.

Thanks to the entire team at Lulu.

Thanks to my Marketing Partners at Watkins Creative Group. Daniel and Holly, you both have been fantastic in helping me start this journey.

I owe a big thank you to my teams at Partners Federal Credit Union and Sharonview Federal Credit Union for all you have done to help me in my ongoing leadership journey.

A special thank you to my Sharonview Board of Directors for your support as the CEO and for your consent to let me chase my dream of writing this book.

Beyond Me
Words and Music by Toby Mckeehan and David Garcia
© 2015 ACHTOBER SONGS (ASCAP), UNIVERSAL MUSIC – BRENTWOOD BENSON PUBLISHING (ASCAP) and D SOUL MUSIC (ASCAP)

ACHTOBER SONGS and UNIVERSAL MUSIC – BRENTWOOD
BENSON PUBLISHING Admin. at CAPITOLCMGPUBLISHING.COM
D SOUL MUSIC Admin. by SPIRIT TWO NASHVILLE
All Rights Reserved   Used by Permission
Reprinted by Permission of Hal Leonard LLC

INTRODUCTION

The Leadership Bet is not a gamble—it's a calculated risk that everything rises and falls on leadership. The outcomes of Sharonview Federal Credit Union, the success of our people, and the way our members (customers) feel about us all rest on the focus of delivering great leadership to our team. This was the bet I made over six years ago when I accepted the CEO job at Sharonview. I had never been a CEO of a credit union up to that point. I decided that I needed to take the risk that placing a premium on leadership could be a difference-making decision on the employees of the credit union and therefore on the then over seventy thousand members who have entrusted $1 billion of their assets to us.

Almost seven years after I started at Sharonview, with more wins than losses due to the bet, I decided to share some of my leadership processes and some stories about my love of this subject called leadership in hopes that this love affair might help some new or aspiring leaders. And maybe there is a thought or two that might even resonate with seasoned leaders.

My leadership journey, which continues to this day, has been a thirty-nine-year adventure filled with ups and downs. Who knows? This story might even encourage you if you don't hold a formal leadership title, but you belong to various groups at a church, a school, or somewhere else where you try to influence others. Simply put, leadership is influence.

What started many years ago as my leadership plan soon developed into my life plan that took in all aspects of who I was and what I believed. I enjoy learning, growing, challenging myself to take some risks, and getting better at what I do every day. My desire has always been to be a lifelong learner and create a better version of myself each day, week, month—you get the picture.

The bet concept is about the idea that career moves involve risks. Heck, simply living involves taking risks. Fear can paralyze us if we let it. Because I had never done a credit union CEO gig before, which involved even more risk for my wife and me because we were moving to a new place for us—Charlotte, North Carolina—and we had no guarantees that leaving Southern California, where I had been born and raised and had spent all fifty-three years of my life to that point, would be successful.

The word *bet* has become an acronym for me.

B = Be disciplined.
E = Execute your plan.
T = Take risks.

This life takes courage, and my philosophy is that you need a foundation of belief in God *and* a belief foundation comprising mentors, best friends, supporters, and truth tellers. The right group of people will spur you on and push you to be your best! Life and leadership involve risks.

We grow when we take risks. We also make that growth more fun if we know what we're passionate about. What really gets you going and excited about what you do? My son told me once that I was lucky because I was doing what I loved and I loved what I was doing. I feel that I figured out early in my career what made me tick was first, helping people, and second, my love of leadership and trying to figure out how this leadership stuff worked and how I could grow my leadership skills. That's a hunt I'm still on today. And the third thing that made me tick was discovering how I could become a better version of Bill today than I was yesterday. That motivated me to do what I needed to do to improve each day.

Have I totally figured it out? Not even close. But the desire to do so makes me better today than I was yesterday. These three passions are what fuel me today. And all three of these works in progress are tied to my day job of leading more than three hundred people every day as the CEO of Sharonview Federal Credit Union.

I made the leadership bet six and a half years ago when Kim and I moved over two thousand miles from Southern California to try this CEO gig out. This leadership stuff is important because good leadership changes lives while great leadership transforms lives, and I want to be a transformer. No, not the movie or the toy, but someone who helps people become the best versions of themselves they can be.

CHAPTER 1
MY DREAM JOB NUMBER 1

I had a dream job at the Walt Disney Company credit union, what I call my dream job number 1. The Partners Federal Credit Union (FCU), was among the top two hundred credit unions in the country (based on asset size) with just over $1 billion in assets.

Growing up in Southern California (So Cal), I became a Disney fan early in life. My family couldn't afford to go to Disneyland a lot, but I got there enough to know that I enjoyed the theme park experience. (I'll date myself now, but does anybody remember the E ticket rides? Back in the 1960s and 1970s, E tickets were for the fast rides like the Matterhorn.) I'm not sure why I gravitated toward Goofy as my favorite character (please don't ask my wife, as you'll probably get a wise guy response); I just really enjoyed the whole park experience. It was always clean, and everyone working there was super nice; it was a huge treat to go to Disneyland! Little did I know that someday I'd be working for one of over three hundred wholly owned subsidiaries of the Walt Disney Company (Partners FCU).

I started developing a real interest in leadership in my mid- to late twenties, and I read all I could get my hands on about Walt Disney—the man behind the mouse. His vision, creativity, and relentless pursuit of his passion inspired me to learn more about him. And while I was a cast member (Disney's term for employee) for the Walt Disney company when I started working for Partners FCU at age forty-five, I had a chance to see up close and personal how Walt put all his passion to work.

What amazed me while I was working for Disney (and it still amazes me today) was the connection almost everyone I talk with has with Disney, Disneyland, or Walt Disney World in Orlando, Florida. Everyone has a story to share about his or her experiences at one of the theme parks or hotels, and it typically revolves around the world-class service. The above-and-beyond stories were numerous, and it's that type of service I wanted to be part of at Partners FCU and wherever I would work from that point on.

One of the best parts of being an insider was the view of the service recovery work that hundreds of cast members took on every day in the parks, at the hotels, or anywhere else that guests met cast members. Disney has a great reputation because they teach their cast members to own the situation where a guest may have experienced poor service, for example, and work to fix the situation. Because Partners was one of 302 wholly owned subsidiaries while I was working there, I had the distinct pleasure of being asked to speak on behalf of the credit union at the Walt Disney Institute to several companies wanting to get Disney's edge in customer service. The credit union was working hard to drive its net promoter scores up across all delivery channels, and I was responsible for creating an environment to deliver Disneyesque service at financial institutions. We developed a very robust closed-loop feedback system that I was able to share with the companies attending the institute—what a blast!

I was the number-two guy at the Disney credit union (depending on the CEO's mood that day; I would joke that I was number three or four if things weren't going well). I was responsible for leading over 50 percent of the credit union staff after about two years at the credit union. As a cast member, I had some terrific benefits. I received a 35 percent discount on merchandise, and I got to attend "Coffee with Bob Iger" (the Disney CEO at the time) at the Burbank studios from time to time. Bob would open up the Walt Disney Studio theater and invite

100–150 cast members over to hear him talk about the company and take questions from the audience. Today, I do "Coffee with Bill," but that may not have the same punch Bob brought to a huge company like Walt Disney.

Also, as a cast member, I had a silver pass that allowed me and three friends (and believe me, you had a lot of friends when they found out you could save them big bucks on park tickets) into the park almost any day of the year.

While I was the senior VP and chief member services officer at Partners, I also had the honor of negotiating with some high-level Disneyland executives to build and open our first Partners' bank branch on Disneyland property. What fun … And what an expensive endeavor! The branch ended up being our most expensive branch ever. I almost had to move our ATM machine after it had been installed because the Disneyland team was sure Walt himself had planted the bushes we needed to remove to meet the ATM building code. Good news—the archives were checked, and the bushes had not been planted by Walt. I mean, I'm a big Walt fan, but he might have cost me $100,000 to move that machine if he had planted them.

I need to share a few more Disney stories. The tunnels at Walt Disney World and the backstage areas at both Disneyland and World were awesome and a little scary. Disney cast members, including the characters, were considered onstage whenever they walked into public areas at the parks. If you had a badge on or a costume, you were expected to be 100 percent in character; only when you made it backstage could you let your guard down. Making my way through the tunnels and backstage at Disneyland, I saw the stuff behind the magic. Let me tell you—when you see Cinderella puffing on a cigarette backstage at Disneyland, it blows the whole magical image thing up a little.

So there I was at my dream job at the Walt Disney credit union. I climbed the ladder to the number-two spot in eight years. I was a cast member with a silver pass. I was living in Southern California, where you could surf in the morning and snow ski in the afternoon. The kids were grown and out of the house, and my wife and I were living in the home I had declared I would be carried out of in my boots. Life was good.

CHAPTER 2
MY POTENTIAL DREAM JOB NUMBER 2

So after eight years at my dream job, I was at the Ballantyne Hotel in South Charlotte, North Carolina, to interview for the chief executive officer (CEO) job for Sharonview Federal Credit Union. It was a Friday afternoon in August 2013, and I was meeting with the board of directors' hiring committee for the credit union later that afternoon. The interview was scheduled for ninety minutes, and besides the hiring committee from the board, it included the existing Sharonview CEO, who was retiring, and the executive recruiter.

The Sharonview CEO job search process had started in April 2013, almost eight years to the month after I had started at Disney, and this was now August. The process was the longest four months of my life! Before I left for the hotel, I got some sage advice from my wife, Kim. "Let the fur fly. Go all in, Bill. Leave it all on the court." The interview could be awkward with the retiring CEO in the room because I was there to talk about how I would make changes to his credit union. I was nervous, but my wife was right (again); I hadn't come that far across the country to be timid or not share what strategies I felt could make a difference at Sharonview. Armed with that great advice, I left for the hotel.

I made my way down a hallway to the hotel lobby, looking for the executive recruiter to get some last-minute words of advice from him as well. He had spent hours with the board of directors, and I knew he could tell me what they were looking for and how to approach them while still being myself. The best advice I thought he had due to the fact he had spent time with me too was to take my time providing answers to their questions. While he didn't tell me the actual questions they would ask, he did share some themes so I'd be prepared. The funny part was that he told me to count to ten before answering a question. Knowing how fast paced I operated, he said, "Just try to get to three before answering." Three was the best he could have hoped for.

The hiring committee was a subset of the full board of directors, which was made up of eleven volunteer board members. I'd read their biographies on the plane and was very impressed. The Sharonview board consisted of a gentleman with a PhD, a retired CFO of a major corporation, a controller for a major corporation, a retired high-ranking human resource professional, two information technology professionals … the list went on. *Wow!* I thought. *These guys and gals are smart, very qualified. I'm in trouble. I'm in over my head.* Sharonview was among the top two hundred credit unions in the United States with impressive financials and a fourteen-year veteran CEO. I became very nervous and started asking myself, *What the heck am I doing?* But to work my way out of my panic attack, I also asked myself, *Why do I want to be a CEO anyway?* something I'd constantly asked myself over the previous four or five years. I was fifty-three at the time and the senior VP and chief member services officer of the Walt Disney credit union; I was living the dream. I had built a great team, I had a supportive boss (the CEO) whom I had known for over twenty years who actually used to work for me at another credit union (more on that later), and I was well paid. And did I mention the silver pass?

The Partners FCU CEO and I had known each other for a long time, and he was one of my original leadership mentors. We used to spend time when we first met twenty-three years earlier; we shared ideas about leadership and what books to read or what tapes (yes, cassette tapes; you young folks might want to google that) to listen to on the drive home. And the entire time I worked for him, he kept throwing challenges at me as I grew bored with my current assignment. He knew me well enough to know that if I got bored, I was going to start looking for something new to do—inside or outside the company.

I had started with Partners FCU as the investment and insurance president. The CEO then added to my duties the oversight of all the credit union branches, and then he gave me the call center though I had had no experience running a call center. He handed me a book written by a so-called expert on running call centers and told me to read it. Then he added, "I got you—you can do this." What a journey the next eighteen months was in figuring that call-center thing out. He then added running the marketing and business development teams to my list of duties.

Each assignment brought about new learning and new leadership work—which I was loving! I was growing and being stretched, experiencing a lot of wins and some losses, and learning from both. But something in me kept wanting to learn more, to try more, to see what else there was to learn and do. The question for me at that point was, *What's the next step on my career path?* For me, it was my boss's job—CEO. Could I do it? Could I lead the entire organization and not just half of it?

Daniel Pink's book *Drive* talks about intrinsic versus extrinsic motivation (Pink 2009). My intrinsic motivation or drive was about challenges, not money or prestige. I really wanted to try this CEO gig out. I had written in my journal in November 2012 that I wanted to be a CEO by 2013. I also kept asking myself why, and the answers were never about money, prestige, or more stuff. The answers always came back to that it was the next step in my lifelong journey of learning. It was my next challenge, and it was possibly my next risk. I had been working for years on becoming the best version of me I could become ("Work harder on yourself than you do on your job"—Jim Rohn), and I was not satisfied with running 50 percent of the organization. My boss and mentor had done all he could do to keep me challenged with new assignments, but we had reached the point that I had topped out at Partners (especially because he told me he wouldn't be leaving anytime soon). As I prayed through my goal of becoming a CEO and after I wrote down the CEO goal in my journal, things started happening.

The other person I need to make you aware of here is my best friend and wife of thirty-eight years, Kim. Besides my CEO friend and mentor, Kim has been my partner in crime for a long time. We met when we were sixteen at a youth group function with the Lakewood Church of Christ. She and her sister were new to the group, and she was (and still is) cute! She also struck me as a self-confident, don't-mess-with-me type of girl. By don't mess with me, I mean we could be friends and have a ton of fun together in a group, but her high standards might make it tough for this So Cal guy (she and her family had moved to So Cal from Montana) to just date for fun. I was (and still am) way out of my league; as I joke with my friends, I outkicked my punt coverage in being lucky enough for her to eventually say yes and marry me in 1982. And here we were, some thirty plus years later having this next step in my career journey. Kim is my Jonathan, Nathan, and Samuel (i.e., Old Testament King David reference—more on that later). You need such foundational relationships in your life to keep you moving, focused, and grounded.

CHAPTER 3
THE TENNESSEE CONNECTION

Several years before I was standing in the Ballantyne Hotel looking for the recruiter, my wife and I were making numerous trips between LA and Nashville, Tennessee, where we would drive two hours to Paris, Tennessee, where our daughter, son-in-law, and two grandsons had moved to from Southern California. My son-in-law was running his family's business from that location and he needed to be at the center of the action. This move left my wife and me 1,500 miles away, whereas we had only been forty-five to sixty minutes away from them before. These trips resulted in our spending time on two-lane country roads and driving past a beautiful lake and through gorgeous countryside. I kept thinking, *I could get used to this*. I was spending two to three hours on the road every day in LA, and I lived only thirty-one miles from my office. In LA, you don't measure time by miles but by minutes or hours to be more realistic.

Prior to our daughter and her family moving to Paris, Tennessee, my wife and I enjoyed living only forty-five minutes east of them and about the same time west of our son and daughter-in-law. We had just moved into the place of our dreams in the foothills, and I really thought we had arrived. We had a lot of extended family in the area, and my job was going very well. And then, the move to Tennessee happened and our world got rocked.

LA was where I had been born and raised. It was crowded, fast-paced, and a great place to live. The weather was almost always awesome. We got our seven inches of rain per year. I'm not sure that's correct, but it wasn't much at all. As I grew older, it seemed that the air was getting cleaner and it was getting hotter. I liked to joke that LA had four seasons: summer, fire, earthquake, and mudslide.

We had smog alerts when I was growing up; when a smog alert was declared, you weren't supposed to do any strenuous physical activity. For me, that meant no recess and no playing kickball, football, or basketball. As kids, we never took that too seriously, but if you did run around too much, you could develop a cough every time you breathed in deeply. It would go away after a good night's sleep, but it got your attention about this thing called smog.

Due to the great weather and the beaches and mountains being close, So Cal was the place to come and live, but all this good stuff led to horrible traffic, high taxes, a high cost of living, and a housing market that was out of control. Homes where we lived were built close together on small lots—six to nine thousand square feet.

CHAPTER 4
WHO IS THIS LA GUY?

I grew up in a normal (I'll let you decide that as you read more), traditional, middle-class family in the LA suburbs. I was the oldest child and had three sisters. Dad was a trailer mechanic, and Mom worked in an office. They worked hard, and we always had clothes to wear and a roof over our heads. I learned from an early age that Dad was a list maker and Mom was the planner/budgeter/you name it of the family. Neither of my parents had gone to college; my dad started to work after he completed eighth grade to help provide for his family of eight brothers and sisters. As I grew older, to-do lists from Dad on Saturdays was the way of life, and they needed to be done by 4:00 p.m., which was when he got home from work.

I always enjoyed figuring out how to most efficiently mow the grass—the best way to push the mower, minimize my steps, and get the most grass bagged in the shortest time. Washing down the driveway … Was it quicker to spray the hose left to the right or right to left? I'm right-handed. I tried to make everything a sort of competition to see how fast I could get it done and looking great. That attitude of mine carried over to anything of a repetitive nature; I've always tried to discover processes to knock out any project as efficiently as possible from stuffing envelopes and making cold calls as a stockbroker to stacking cardboard boxes at my summer job in high school. Side note here—everyone should work in a cardboard factory during his or her junior year of high school—it was there that I cemented the thought that I was going to college. I became the first person in my family to earn a BA.

That took me seven years because I'd fallen in love with Kim and started working full time to support our family, but I did it.

My dad's mom (she told us to call her Nana because she wasn't old enough to be a grandma) came to live with us when I was in sixth grade. She had the faith of Moses, and she made sure we held what we called church services on weeknights. She gave us short lessons, and we sang hymns a cappella.

She and our mom found a Church of Christ a few miles away, and we began attending there regularly; that was my introduction to God. Nana and Mom were strong believers. Though he was a believer, Dad wasn't interested in church attendance during that season of his life, but he made it clear that we didn't get to stay home with him on Sundays; we were all required to go to church. I was baptized within the first year we began attending the church, and my faith began to take shape when I was a young teenager. I'll save all my learnings, failures, and bad choices for another book. Suffice it to say that I've been on a journey with God for quite a while and that He was the reason I was able to make my leadership bet.

I loved spending time with my nana when I was young. She was one of the biggest Los Angeles Dodgers fans I knew. We would listen to many games with the voice of Vince Scully on the radio, and if my memory serves me right, she taught me how to keep score of a baseball game. It wasn't below her to fuss at the team if they weren't playing well, and she developed in me a lifelong love of baseball in general and the Dodgers in particular.

My biggest issue now is that living on the East Coast and following a West Coast team is not conducive to getting a good night's sleep. I thank Google and Major League Baseball for offering highlights of the games the following morning.

As I was finishing up my second year of junior college, I decided to start a list of my goals. I would have loved to attend the University of Southern California (USC), but I didn't have the money, grades, or SAT scores to even consider getting in there. If you lived in LA, you talked about only two schools, and everyone had a favorite—USC or UCLA. I'm not sure exactly why, but I gravitated toward USC, and as fate would have it, that gravitation played a role in my marrying a young woman whose grandfather had graduated from USC in 1935. While attending junior college, my running joke about going to Cerritos College, which was on Alondra Boulevard in Cerritos, was that I was going to UCLA—the *University of Cerritos Left on Alondra*.

I made my first goal list some forty years ago as I attended my particular UCLA, and I still have that list. I discovered that making a goal list helped me focus on my goals and lifted a weight off my shoulders by allowing me to clear my head and focus on the tasks at hand. I'd look back during the year and in the years to follow and was amazed to see what I had accomplished. I learned how powerful of a tool it was to set goals in writing. David Allen's book *Getting Things Done* talks about the power of writing down your goals and clearing up some thinking space (Allen 2001). Jim Rohn spends a chapter in his book *Seven Strategies for Wealth and Happiness* on the importance of goal setting, and he gives practical advice on ways to set up goals (Rohn 1996).

In my thirties, I set up an individual development plan (IDP), what many call a personal development plan. I tried different ways to capture areas I wanted to improve in, but I never really settled on the best tool to use. I finally latched on to Excel and began creating a notebook with various tabs to list my goals looking forward a year and longer, and that notebook began to grow.

About ten years later, I started journaling. I was not a faithful journal user at first, but it began to grow on me. My journal, my prayer life, and my individual or personal development plan started to make a difference in how I felt about becoming the best version of me I could become. I then had a way to track my progress.

One note on using a journal here ... Your journal is yours; no one gets to tell you how to journal or what to write in it. I feared making a mistake in my journal as I was writing out an idea or capturing notes or whatever, but I overcame that. It was mine alone. I like to call it my idea catcher, and I have even doodled in it to help me create a new department or two at our credit union or develop some initial thinking and idea points about how to move the organization from here to there. It has been an invaluable tool for me, and I'm still perfecting my journaling.

I was always on the hunt for a process to make all this work. I was sure that someone out there had to have thought of this before me. What was the formula to be successful and impactful to those around me and my family? How should all this work? I used trial and error and studied and researched how great leaders did what they did. I wanted a repeatable and sustainable process to chart my course and track my progress. (For some views of what I use to this day for my IDP and my life plan, see the link in footnote [1] below.)

I started my career in financial services in 1980 at age twenty as a drive-up teller at a branch that was robbed about every six months; we were freeway-close for our robber friends. I immediately fell in love with the whole concept of banking. I discovered that this was a place to work a process, figure out ways to make it better, and create efficiencies in how fast I could service

---

[1] Go to www.theleadershipbet.com for an IDP or life plan.

customers and balance my teller cash drawer. My trainer had a foolproof process to ensure that my teller drawer was never out of balance, which meant I got to try learning other areas of the bank.

It was there that I also discovered my passion for helping people. I loved helping customers with their money matters, and I was promoted to a new accounts clerk position during my first year there. I thoroughly enjoyed connecting our customers' money with their plans. And since I balanced my teller cash drawer perfectly for an entire year, I was able to leave the branch to head into the management development program.

I'd had a couple of early wins from a career perspective—one was my love of helping people, and the other was that through the management development program, I'd discovered that I was okay at managing people. My operations officer identified me as someone "with potential," and he encouraged me to apply for the management development program. He was a huge advocate for me and unselfishly helped me learn as much as I could absorb in the year I was at his branch. Another of my early wins was learning the importance of having someone in your corner, a mentor to help you see in yourself what you might not have realized was right there in front of you.

During that time, I was lucky enough to marry that Kim I'd mentioned earlier. We were twenty-two when we got married, and I felt extremely lucky to have her in my life and on my journey. I was working my seven-year plan trying to finish my bachelor's degree from California State University at Long Beach, but during work hours, I was a sponge soaking up any new assignments I could get my hands on. I wasn't afraid to try moving to new branches and meeting new staff members. I enjoyed the challenge that presented, and I was prone to getting bored without new challenges being placed in front of me.

Another one of my big early learnings was that my leader wasn't scared to lose his top performer. He kept me fired up, engaged, and asking for more responsibility and more challenges. His openness to recognizing this in me and allowing me to leave the nest has stayed with me my entire career, and I believe this may have been my first encounter with servant leadership. This is something I try to do to this day; I work to recognize the talents my people possess, help them develop those talents to their fullest, and have an abundance mentality that isn't afraid to lose them if they decide to move on up or outside our organization. My belief is that this frame of mind creates highly engaged and motivated employees who will run through walls for you.

My seven-year plan to earn a BA in finance also saw me go from teller to vice president in six years. Just as every college student who finishes a degree in finance thinks, I thought it was time for me to become a stockbroker. When I graduated in 1985, I was already on my way to becoming a VP of operations at a small commercial bank, but I dreamed of becoming a stockbroker and getting back to my roots—my desire to help people.

When I lost my job at the bank in 1986, I was propelled into a frantic search to see if I could fulfill my dream of becoming a stockbroker. Losing my job came at a bad time, but isn't that the case with all job losses? Kim and I had just bought a home in La Mirada, and she had just delivered our second child. He had some medical issues that required medication and more doctor visits than normal that cost money with or without insurance. Losing my job was a real blow to my self-esteem. I'd felt I was invincible. I'd climbed the corporate ladder from teller to VP in commercial banking in six years. That moment in my life was not only a setback for my career; it was also humbling and frustrating.

And a new mortgage, a second child, and no money coming in put us in a place I'd never wish on anybody.

Regardless, we jumped into action and had faith that God would see us through—but we had to do our part in His plan. I washed cars and did all kinds of odd jobs as I searched for work. Kim was my sanity check; she supported us in all kinds of ways including managing our growing family.

I did indeed find a stockbroker job that would allow me to get back to helping individuals fulfilling their dreams with investments. I had done my research, and I'd interviewed a stockbroker; I thought I could handle the job. *How hard could it be?* I asked myself. I was fortunate enough to be hired by Dean Witter in late 1986. I was given a bread-and-water salary and was told that if I didn't pass the Series 7 (General Securities Representative) exam, I wouldn't work for the firm any longer. I was to take that test four months from my start date. If I passed that exam, I'd take the Series 63 (Uniform Securities State Agent) and then the California insurance license exams.

I passed all the exams and started producing, as they called it, in April 1987. Being a stockbroker was much different from what my interview had led me to believe. I remember walking back into the office after a month of training in New York. (Dean Witter had a series of floors in one of the World Trade Center towers that were demolished on 9/11.) After spending four weeks with 127 other new stockbrokers, I was shown to my bullpen cubicle, handed my business cards and a phone, and was wished good luck in starting my business.

My game plan was to work with individual investors and work particular wealthy areas in Downey and Lakewood, California. Here's where that process orientation would come into play again. I would make a hundred cold calls or dials per day for three years. On many occasions, my bullpen mates and I would make a thousand dials in one day starting with businesses in the morning and moving on to personal residences in the afternoon and into the evening. I'm quite sure that I was one of many reasons the Federal Communications Commission put its Do Not Call list into play.

I wasn't a good stockbroker based on my commission earnings, but I learned a lot during my three years in the business. Number one: I learned how to persevere when really all I wanted to do was not dial the phone anymore. Number two: I found out what an unbelievable support system I had in my wife, who had basically told me to give Dean Witter a try because I would always second-guess myself if I didn't take this shot at living out my college dream of becoming a stockbroker. She calls this her woulda shoulda coulda philosophy. Number three: I could indeed convince some of those I called to let me mail them some material regarding the investment ideas I was pitching. I'd schedule them for a callback hoping to schedule a meeting with them at their homes. I considered myself a kitchen-table dude who preferred to meet my potential clients on their home turf.

The formula was that a hundred cold calls or dials would result in thirty-five or so contacts that would result in mailing out five to seven packets of information. The callbacks would generally result in setting three appointments, but for the most part, one kept appointment would be the result.

What I discovered was that the people who did meet with me were fantastic and that many of them needed help with their investments or their investment planning. At Dean Witter, I was able to reconnect with my passion for helping people.

With my training, I was able to do some good for those who allowed me, a new, young buck broker, into their homes. Back then, I was driving a beat-up 1980 Toyota Celica; doesn't that just say, "You're dealing with a very successful stockbroker"? The metallic molding on the passenger side windshield was loose and would flap in the wind if I went over thirty mph. I was so embarrassed that I'd park seven to eight houses down the street and walk to the potential clients' houses so they wouldn't see my lousy car.

With only our next mortgage payment in our savings account, I decided that my three-year journey as a stockbroker needed to end and that I needed to get a real job. That was when I was introduced to credit unions; in 1989, I took a job at Lockheed Federal Credit Union in Burbank, California.

Kim supported our family for those three years as my Dean Witter salary had only a one-year guarantee; after that, I was on 100 percent commission. She not only supported our family; she also allowed me to chase my dream of being a stockbroker. Everyone needs a Kim! She's my truth teller, a call-me-on-my-stuff person. She has always listened to my ideas, dumb or otherwise, and then she challenges my thinking, and then she's 100 percent in my corner all the time unconditionally—no matter what. She's the reason we survived while I chased my dream of being a stockbroker. She's the reason we bought several homes and upgraded our home with every move we made in Southern California. She's the reason I went for the interview with Sharonview and as she tells it "drug her across country" to move to Charlotte. She's why I went into the interview and let it fly even though the retiring CEO was in the room. She was and is my Samuel (my spiritual guide), my Jonathan (my best friend) and my Nathan (my truth teller) packed into a wonderful, five-one package that has tolerated me for thirty-eight years and counting.

She's supported my career dreams and midlife crisis, though she'd tell you I had several midlife crises. One included wanting a convertible, a Honda S-2000. I ended up with a Mazda Miata thanks to Kim. Need I say more?

I needed a job with a salary and decided to go back into banking, but I wanted to keep my securities licenses; I had worked hard for them and believed they might serve a purpose down the road though I had no idea what. Keeping my licenses might have been a challenge ten years earlier, but brokers had started working for banks and these things called credit unions, which had a mantra—people helping people—something that fit with my passion for doing exactly that. Banks and credit unions alike were offering retirement planning, college planning, and all the products and services I had been trained to sell while I was at Dean Witter.

I put some applications in and was hired as a discount stockbroker at Lockheed Federal Credit Union. There, I met and hired someone who later mentored me at Partners FCU. I worked in Burbank for eighteen years at Lockheed and Partners.

A credit union, as I learned, was a financial institution that was a not-for-profit financial cooperative. That's a fancy way of saying that credit unions were owned by their members and were in existence for their benefit alone. Credit unions don't have stockholders, and they don't pay federal or state taxes, which allows them to return more of the members' money to them by offering higher rates on savings products and lower rates on loans than the typical for-profit bank offered. The people-helping-people concept had gotten me started in my career, and I was able to keep all my securities licenses—a win-win for me. Well, a win-win-win in that I then had a salaried job and was no longer on 100 percent commission.

CHAPTER 5
MY DREAM JOB NUMBER 2

The interview for the Sharonview CEO job was over. I left The Ballantyne hotel and drove back to our hotel. My wife asked how it had gone, and I told her that I liked the board members. As I interviewed them while letting the fur fly, they came across as smart, sincere volunteers who were interested in changing the way things were being done at the credit union.

My interview had lasted two hours versus the ninety-minutes it had been scheduled for, and as I shared with my wife how it had gone, I became excited about the possibilities. Then reality set in. I was the first of six potential candidates who would parade in front of the hiring committee. I thought that with my lack of credit union CEO experience, I was just interview bait, or someone the recruiter could throw in front of the hiring committee to fill out the slate of candidates. *This job's way over my head and too big for me*, I thought. *This would be a good practice run for a CEO job, but there was no way these smart board members would take the crazy, bald-headed guy from Southern California seriously.* In fact, that's what I had told my boss at Partners and Kim.

Because I didn't want to bank (sorry for the bad pun, but I'm a credit union guy) on the Sharonview job and since I had felt early in the recruiting process that this was just a great way to learn how this recruiting thing worked, I had also applied for the CEO role at a credit union in Tennessee with another recruiting firm.

As I made my way through the Sharonview CEO process, I was simultaneously working my way through the Oak Ridge, Tennessee, CEO job search. I guess you could say I was not putting all my eggs in one basket. The Oak Ridge job was at a credit union named Y-12, which was roughly half the size of Sharonview. I had made my way through their hiring process and was one of two finalists when I had flown with Kim to Charlotte and interviewed for the CEO job at Sharonview. While I felt I was in way over my head for the Sharonview CEO role, I felt confident that I could do the job and be a difference maker at Y-12. In my mind, I could handle the $600 million Y-12 on my own, but I had no idea how I would handle the $1 billion Sharonview. And that's the major point of this story—I couldn't have without God's help.

The Y-12 board seemed a little stiff to me at the first in-person interview; before the board members would ask me a question, they would look at the chairman to see if he was good with their asking a question. It was kind of crazy, but I was willing to give the final go-around a chance and see if my crazy antenna was still up after the presentation, which included an informal gathering with the full board after the presentation. I was one of two finalists for the Y-12 CEO role; the presentation and informal gathering was scheduled for the week after the Sharonview interview. Y-12 was close to the University of Tennessee, so Kim outfitted me in a super cool orangish tie that worked with my money suit. I jokingly referred to that suit as my money suit because it was the most expensive one I'd ever bought. It had cost $700—cheap by some suit standards, but I was a Men's Wearhouse kind of guy. Kim made sure that I could dress it up with different shirt/tie combinations, and she really made it work for any interview.

After explaining how the Sharonview had gone, I told Kim, "Let's get out of here and head home." I needed to get my PowerPoint presentation finished for the job I thought I could handle in Tennessee. We were leaving the following week for

Tennessee to see the kids and grandkids in Paris after heading to Oak Ridge, where I'd give my presentation. She politely told me that I should buzz off, that we were staying in Charlotte until it was time to fly home the next afternoon, a Saturday. She said, "You've drug me across the entire country to do this interview, and now it's time to see some sights." So we did some sightseeing and had a great dinner. She's very smart and almost always right … That was another of those moments. We flew back to LA Saturday afternoon, and I found myself in my Partners FCU office in Burbank on Sunday morning finishing up my presentation for the Tennessee interview.

About 10:30 that morning, I received a text from the executive recruiter for the Sharonview CEO role: "They're going to offer you the CEO job at Sharonview." "I'll be in touch" was how he finished it. I immediately texted back, "Wait a minute. You said the board was interviewing five other candidates and would invite back the top two to do a presentation to the full board and then the board would make its selection." "They didn't need to do that," he texted. "They were sold that you were their guy."

I sat in my office in the state of shock not knowing what to do. I had told Kim through every step of the way from April 2013 until then, August, that we could always say no if we were lucky enough to continue beyond the practice run. LA had been Kim's home for thirty-seven years and mine for all my life. I had fifty-three years invested there in family, friends, church, homes, schools—everything. This was a big deal. Now we were supposed to pick up and leave everything we had worked for and been blessed with by God and move all the way across the country? My questions ranged from *Does Charlotte know about the Pac-12?* to *Can I do this huge job?* and everything in between. I felt sick. I texted Kim that I was coming home, that we needed to talk. The recruiter had assumed that we were taking the job. At eleven that Sunday morning, I wouldn't have given you odds about that happening.

I drove home in a fog. Hundreds of thoughts raced through my mind—excitement, fear, wow, fear, oh crap, awesome—they ran the gamut. I got home, and we started talking about everything. We decided to pray about it and not make a decision right away. And at that point, I hadn't even asked how much this CEO gig paid.

On Monday morning, I asked my boss, the CEO of Partners FCU, if we could talk. When Kim okayed my looking for a CEO job in other parts of the country, I'd gone public with my boss about the possibility. I'd never done that over my thirty-three-year career before, but I decided I wanted his counsel, his insights, and his blessing. I trusted him after all the time we'd spent talking about leadership and sharing our dreams with each other. He'd invited me to play Monday-morning quarterback after our monthly board meetings and ask any questions I had about the meetings.

So because of our twenty-three-year history and lifelong learners' mindsets, I talked with him to let him know what I was considering doing. If he wasn't okay with it, I'd need to sneak around and try to make this big career move on my own. Kim was my rock, but I also needed my mentor and industry insider. Who better than the guy who had been one of my original mentors and would give me straight-up feedback about my progress based on my sharing of the journey and milestones I had hit along the way?

I told him the entire story about the weekend in Charlotte. Just to be clear, I had disclosed to him a few months earlier that I was going after the Sharonview job, and he also knew about the Tennessee finalist gig coming up later that same week. We were leaving on Wednesday, and I wasn't sure what to do at that point. Kim and I still had not made any call on go or no go regarding Sharonview.

My CEO friend and mentor offered me some good advice. He asked me if I had the official offer letter in my hand from Sharonview. I told him no. He said that until such time, he would recommend that I continue my efforts with the Tennessee credit union. He said that things could change and that if the verbal offer from the recruiter never resulted in a written offer from the board, I had nothing legally binding at that point. He reminded me that we had already planned on seeing our daughter, son-in-law, and grandkids in Tennessee anyway, so he told us to head on out and give my presentation.

He laughed and said, "Wouldn't it be ironic if you knocked the Tennessee presentation out of the park and ended up with two credit union offers to consider?" He high-fived me and sent me on my way. I talked to Kim about this strategy, and she was game to give it a try. We continued talking to God and each other; we didn't tell anyone else what was happening.

I finished preparing my Tennessee presentation, and we left town on Wednesday. We landed in Nashville and rented a car to head to the Tennessee credit union town of Oak Ridge. The presentation was the next day, and we were on I-40 headed toward Knoxville when I got a text from the Sharonview recruiter; he wanted me to check my email. I did. There it was. The offer letter. We pulled over at a rest stop, and I read it to Kim. Pay, benefits, bonus plan, vacation, you name it, it was in there. We were shocked and just sat there for a while. This was a top-tier credit union making an offer to the number two (or three or four) guy at the Disney credit union with no credit union CEO experience. They wanted us to move across the country, where we knew exactly five people (our nephew and his wife and three kids in Raleigh, NC, three hours north of Charlotte) and lead two hundred employees to the next level.

Kim and I spent the next twenty to thirty minutes going over all the pros and cons. We rehashed previous discussions, but this was real. I had told Kim all along that we were in the driver's seat and could say no at any time. If it was too risky, or we just didn't want to leave our family and friends, or any of the other seven hundred reasons we had to just stay put in LA, we could just say no thanks. I was shocked, humbled, and scared all at once as I stared at the letter.

When I tell you that you need a Kim in your life, I mean you need someone who in that moment at a rest stop on I-40 would look you in the eyes and say, "I never want you to say, 'I wish I would've done this.'" She had told me the same thing several times in my career, one when I took the Dean Witter job, one when I took a broker-dealer job I'd had no business taking due to my lack of experience, and then at a rest stop on I-40. Kim said, "I don't want you to say woulda shoulda coulda." In spite of the confusion, excitement, and nervousness, she was giving me the go-ahead to rip our lives up in Southern California and move 2,600 miles east to Charlotte. We said one more prayer together and then shouted, "Let's head east!"

As we talked at that rest stop, it hit me how much I wanted this big job, but I wondered if I could handle it. There was a lot of risk, but I was excited at the challenge. The Tennessee job was very doable I thought, but the Sharonview job had me worried. I had no idea even where to start with it. But that was exactly where God wanted me—dependent on Him and in the deep end of the pool so I would know who was in control and who was pulling the strings.

Once we agreed that this was the job, we wondered about what to do about the Tennessee interview. We talked some more, and I knew I couldn't just show up and not tell my other recruiter, who knew nothing about my interviewing in Sharonview, about this miracle we had just been part of on I-40. I was now at an ethical corner. *Should I just show up and do the presentation and not say anything, or should I come clean and let the Tennessee recruiter know that I just got what I considered the job offer of a lifetime and wouldn't be a finalist for the Tennessee job?*

We talked more on the drive to Oak Ridge and over dinner at an Applebee's before heading to the hotel. Kim and I agreed that the right thing to do was to let the Tennessee recruiter know what was going on. I called him and told him that we were in Oak Ridge and that I would deliver the presentation of a lifetime, I said, to the Tennessee board, but because I wanted to try the big job at Sharonview, I wouldn't be accepting a Y-12 job offer if I was fortunate enough to receive one. I felt this would leave the recruiter in a good spot as he had another qualified candidate available for the job, so if I bowed out after the presentation, the other guy could be the victor.

Based on his reaction, I thought that he considered that the dumbest idea ever presented to him in all his years of recruiting. He let me know that I would not be presenting the next day and that he had never been in a situation like that before in his career. He basically hung up on me. I really found it hard to believe that no one had ever conducted multiple job searches with two separate recruiters, but we got back into the car and headed back to Paris, Tennessee, to see the kids and grandkids.

We spent a few days with the kids and grandkids, and we shared the story with our kids. Kim and I negotiated with Sharonview on a few items in the offer letter, but overall, the offer was extremely generous, and I remember walking through a Target in Clarksville, Tennessee, when Kim and I agreed to the final version of the offer letter. I accepted the offer, and we started making plans to attend Sharonview's annual strategic planning conference in Hilton Head in mid-September. It was late August, so I had a lot of work to do to get ready to depart my Disney credit union job.

CHAPTER 6
MY LEADERSHIP JOURNEY

My leadership journey had begun in 1981 at age twenty-one. Or should I say my management journey began then. I don't think I thought much about leadership at that point. I was very rules and regulations oriented and extremely numbers driven, which fit perfectly with being a bank's operations officer. I could quote you book, chapter, and verse on what rule applied to what section of the policy and procedures manual or what we all affectionately called the PPM. I enjoyed working with a team then, and I probably had just enough emotional intelligence to get by at age twenty-one.

    I also had learned a decent amount of positive thinking from my mom and my soon-to-be wife as my life coach to be an effective supervisor. I was a decent listener, a problem solver, and I was a high E (based on the Myers-Briggs scale), an extrovert—I got my energy through processing out loud and working in groups. I enjoyed leading others to create shared wins. Some of that might have traced back to the Mayfair Monsoons, my high school basketball team, one of the best teams in 2-A California Interscholastic Foundation (CIF) in Southern California in 1978. I was not quite six feet tall, but my driver's license said I was six feet. (I'd put that down when I got my first driver's license, and the staffer at the DMV hadn't demanded that I prove it.) I averaged 2.5 points a game; I wasn't a prolific scorer to say the least, but I could play defense with the best of them and loved to feed the ball to my six-seven friend. I got more joy out of a great dish or assist than scoring a bucket. What is that old John Wooden saying, "It takes ten hands to score a basket"? (Wooden 2009). My two hands were usually involved in passing the ball or defending against someone who was trying to score.

By the time I'd finished my commercial banking career some five years later, I had risen to the VP level. That was 1986, and I had learned that I enjoyed managing people, but I hadn't figured out this leadership thing yet. I had graduated a year earlier from California State University in Long Beach with a degree in finance at age twenty-five. As I mentioned, it took me seven years to earn it because I started working full time before Kim and I married, and I took classes part time. I'd really wanted to put that degree to work after I graduated, and that led to my stint as a stockbroker.

During my three years at Dean Witter, I wasn't concerned with growing my management skills or reading a lot of books; I was trying just to survive month to month. I wasn't working on any theory of leadership, but I was logging hours and hours of practical learning about how to persevere, how to create leads, and to celebrate a lot of small victories while staring down the negativity of starting at zero every month. All the time I was there, I still had this sense that I was there to simplify the complex—to be able to talk about investments with everyday people and therefore helping them. I never lost that key driver of wanting to help people even though my wife was supporting our family financially while I was barely helping cover the mortgage.

In 1990, as I mentioned, I hired someone at Lockheed FCU who became my first mentor. We were almost the same age, but he was a real student of leadership. We'd talk for hours it seemed about ideas and concepts involving leadership and the differences between leadership and management. He was the one who introduced me to Jim Rohn, a business philosopher. I wasn't sure what that meant, but I listened to one of his books on tape, bought a series of CDs in which Rohn and other speakers talked about leadership, and read one of his books. He ties a lot of his material to wealth, but he offers many great life and leadership lessons. I decided I would finally try to put together an individual development plan, an IDP, that would work for me. I had been trying to find one off the shelf but had never found one that worked for me.

Around that same time, I started thinking that I had one of the greatest mentors anyone could ask for—Jesus. I was and still am a big Jesus fan, and I felt He was one of the greatest leaders ever. One of the best ideas my first mentor gave me was the idea that the best way to become a great leader or great anything else is to study those who have become or are great leaders. I began to read books about great leaders—Ronald Reagan, Lee Iacocca, General MacArthur, Walt Disney, John Wooden, the Bible, Benjamin Franklin—and my library began to grow. Reading those books prompted many questions: What did they do that made themselves great? How did they react to controversy? How did they create a following? What was their story? How did they handle success? More important, how did they handle failure? I was also building my individual development plan on an Excel spreadsheet to track certain items.

Thanks to Rohn, I became more intentional about getting ideas on how to grow as a leader from sermons, seminars, conferences, books, books on tape (literally on cassette tape—no Audible account then), and any other way I could cram data into my head about how to become the best version of Bill I could become. I wrote down the best ideas I came across at first on paper and then in a journal ... sort of. I really didn't do a good job of capturing my learnings until I was in my forties. From age thirty to thirty-three, I was getting back into management at Lockheed

FCU starting as a supervisor and then quickly rising to manager. It was there that I met my second mentor. He was a tough-minded, former police officer who had become our CFO. He taught me some hard lessons about budgeting that I use to this day. He was a great storyteller, and he could sniff out BS quicker than anyone I'd ever met. He was a good listener, and he asked great questions all the time.

He also gave me some very good advice a time or two. One piece of advice was about my desire to get either an MBA or a CFP (certified financial planner) designation. He asked me, "What do you really want to do when you grow up?" That forced me to ask myself if I wanted to lead people (for which an MBA would be better) or if I wanted to lead clients to their financial goals (for which a CFP would pay huge dividends). After thinking about both paths, I decided that I really enjoyed leading people more, so I decided to get an MBA, which took me two years; I was thirty-five when I made that goal a reality.

Let me take a detour here. I believe in higher education not for the piece of paper you get at the end but for the mind-widening capabilities it provides to help you look at situations, opportunities, and issues from different points of view. I'd had the good fortune of working for a bank in my early career that had a tuition reimbursement program; the bank literally paid for my undergraduate degree. Lockheed also had a tuition reimbursement program that paid for almost 80 percent of my MBA. And since I got straight A's in all my MBA classes (Please know that I lived the C's get degrees thing during my undergraduate years), I requested the other 20 percent of my MBA expenses … and got it! I believe my MBA helped me land the Sharonview job not for the resume fodder it provided but for the experience the MBA opportunity had provided me with working in high-performing groups and delivering some pretty unique research papers. One of those projects landed our group in front of the LA County Sheriff's Department top dog doing a community policing presentation.

I worked full time and went to school one to two nights a week for my MBA, and that was tough on our family and especially on our kids, who were nine and seven when I started the MBA program. Kim was working two nights a week teaching painting. We literally passed each other Tuesdays and Thursdays; I'd walk into the house as she was heading out to her community college campus. On Mondays and Wednesdays, I worked "half days" starting at 7:00 a.m. and then heading to class after work, usually from 6:00 p.m. to 10:00 p.m. Crazy! But the degree really paid off. My reading habits improved during that time as you can imagine. I didn't read much on leadership those days, but I had to create time and space to get my homework done and still make sure there was time for the kids while their mom was teaching. Life was busy to say the least.

From 1995 to 2004, I continued to read, gather ideas, and take some notes, but I still had no great formula for keeping it all straight. I'd had a goal list since 1980, when I was twenty, but I hadn't figured out how to store the ideas I'd captured in a way I could retrieve and study them so I could use them in a meaningful way.

I did however continue grabbing anything I could get my hands on about leadership and great leaders. I started developing some favorite authors and preachers, and I was still impressed by this Jesus character. John Maxwell, Jim Collins, John Wooden, and Patrick Lencioni became favorites of mine during that time. The Bible has always been a top read for me too. I believe it has created a good balance for me to read earthly authors and the

Bible. There are so many scriptures that get directly or indirectly referenced in the books I read; it wasn't a coincidence.

About the time I turned thirty, I had an Excel workbook that helped me keep stuff organized by tabs. On one tab, I divided my goals lists into areas that made sense for me—spiritual goals, fitness goals, career goals, family goals, travel goals, and so on. The next tab listed all the books I had read. I did the same for my health; I tracked the important numbers—cholesterol, blood pressure, triglycerides, glucose—the major items from my annual physical.

These components or tabs in my spreadsheet began to take shape, and I updated them easily. If I ran across an idea I wanted to access later, I'd make a note on a tab that I had created called Great Questions and Learning. It felt good to finally have a home for the different aspects of my life that I wanted to keep track of. (See footnote [2] for more on my life plan.) I also began listing whom I was being influenced by, mentors, coaching ideas for my teams and me, and what I was going to focus on the year. How was I planning on growing my skills and abilities as a leader? Where would I spend my time? What were the next big ideas I wanted to research? How would I go about researching them? That became my individual development plan.

During my almost ten years at Lockheed Federal Credit Union (now LOGIX), I got involved with an executive coach for the first time. During 1993, this industrial psychologist was brought in, and she had us take some tests, which we debriefed about in a classroom setting with other managers. That was where I learned the power of getting feedback from those I worked with. We had a session during which we shared the impact other managers had on us individually. It was powerful to learn how each of us was

---

[2] See www.theleaderhipbet.com.

perceived at work. I remember thinking, *I had no idea that's how I was impacting him/her.* I knew that from that point forward, I was going to do a better job of sharing my feedback with, and asking for feedback from those I worked with.

We also met with the industrial psychologist one on one for individual coaching. She provided managers with books to read based on their individual profiles, and she helped interpret their test results and determine how they could maximize their God-given talents. The three books she gave me are still on my shelf.

That experience shaped my thinking about executive coaching. I have been working with an executive coach since 2007, and I've been fortunate enough to have had the same coach for almost ten years. She's a PhD, and she calls me on my stuff. She pushes me to think, she pushes me to new heights, and she does what any good coach does … she forces me to do the work. Her guidance, her great questions, and her insight have helped me become a better executive.

From 1981 to today, I have been on a journey—a leadership journey. I just soak up ideas and try things out. I would test the theories I was reading and learning about along with trying some good old trial-and-error methodology or as I like to say, on-the-job training. During this time, I began to realize that the powerful combination of developing relationships and delivering results was the deal maker. Relationships needed to be cultivated in all directions—up, on a peer level, across the organization regardless if folks formally reported to me or not, and throughout my downline. I spent time developing my leadership operating system, a series of short statements and concepts that could stand on their own or as a group of ideas that would encourage an individual to stay the course of leadership.

Over time, these short statements grew into what I now call my leadership guiding principles. They're not new, but when used in combination, they can create a powerful environment that can produce excellent results and a great place to work with other people.

CHAPTER 7
LEADERSHIP GUIDING PRINCIPLES

Principle 1—Work harder on yourself than you do on your job.

Jim Rohn (1996) coined this phrase, and I believe this is the number-one principle of great leaders and great persons. Great is a strong word, but it's the working toward being great at something that makes a difference. It means having the discipline to do the things I need to do to get better and better, learning, growing, and trying new things and ways to do them all the time. Working harder on myself than I do on my job allows me to become the best version of Bill I can be. And that means my wife, my kids, my grandkids, my employer, and my friends get to see and experience a better Bill than they knew the day before.

This principle means that my life is in balance. In December 2007, my boss at Partners FCU sent me to the Center for Creative Leadership (CCL) in Colorado. He wanted to send some of his high-performing leaders to a program he had attended there called Leadership at the Peak. I was forty-seven when I went to CCL, and the experience changed my life as a leader. The assessments, the personal executive coaching, the high caliber of attendees (the class was limited to eleven people from around the country and from all walks of life and industries), the exercises (physical and mental) all came together over five days, and those who attended completely understood how to take our leadership game to the next level. It was expensive but worth every penny the credit union paid (at least in my opinion)!

CCL describes it using four small circles representing areas of our lives—self, family, career, and community—surrounded by one large circle. If our lives are in balance, each of our smaller circles should be the same size. But at times, one area of our lives might be larger than another or getting more airtime than the other areas; over time, such domination could rob us of experiences that would make our lives fuller.

The larger circle represents the spiritual aspect of our lives, and for me, this is God. The self, family, and career circles are self-explanatory. The community circle represents the social part of my life—my friends, coworkers, and acquaintances.

Working harder on me than I do on my job means I want to be a lifelong learner. I read books, listen to books on Audible and podcasts, network, surf the web to research whatever interests me, listen to good music, and attend conferences focused on leadership and personal development. I watch webinars and good movies, take in good sermons, and read the Bible. Being around people who stretch me and make me think is important to being a lifelong learner.

Try this exercise; it might tell you a lot about where you may be headed. Ask yourself who the top three to five people you spend the most time with are. I enjoy all kinds of ways to learn, and I try to make learning a priority. And I believe you can learn something from almost anyone. When I was twenty-six, I worked for a guy who wore the crispest white cotton shirts; he looked like he might have a heart attack at any moment. He was all about the business and didn't have any time for this people stuff. I remember putting into my mental rolodex that I would never treat people as he did. (See principle 2 regarding developing relationships.)

Working harder on myself means I cannot compartmentalize my life, because I am a complete person. Years ago, I wanted to keep everything separate—my church life, my home life, my work life—like a child's plate with dividers—but I learned that that was impossible to pull off and not very healthy. Plus, it was exhausting! Now, I strive to be an authentic, whole person. WYSIWYG—What You See Is What You Get. The more I read and study about leadership, the more I am convinced that the leaders people enjoy following are ethical and authentic, the type people gravitate to and follow.

This principle also means that I need to be physically fit. If I feel good, that will spill over into all aspects of my life. I will be more productive at work, at home, and in every area of my life. This also means eating right. Taking care of myself allows me to take care of those I love and care about. A ton of research is out there about the benefits everyone can derive from being physically fit. The Center for Creative Leadership program I attended spent a fair amount of time on this subject, and I've incorporated this aspect of leadership development into our Sharonview leadership program.

I mentioned playing for my high school team, the Mayfair Monsoons. My six-seven friend was a great scorer; that year, he was named the coplayer of the year in our state division. What an honor for him and our team! I found out a few years after we left high school that he used to work out early in the morning each day before most of us teammates even got out of bed. I thought he was naturally gifted, and he was, but he worked to improve the gift God had given him to take his game to new heights. He was offered a full-ride basketball scholarship to a Pac-12 school; how awesome is that? Finding this out let me know that it was one thing to find your gift or gifts, but it was another to have the discipline to use and improve them to become great.

If I were a golfer, and I'm not, I'd follow this first principle by focusing not on how the others in my foursome were doing but on how I was doing. I decided long ago to quit looking around at what gifts or skills others had and focus on improving what gifts God had given me; I wanted to focus on improving my own game. I still always compete against myself to become a better listener, a better communicator, a better husband, and so on. John Wooden said, "You always win when you make the full effort to do the best of which you are capable" (Wooden 2009).

Principle 2—Develop relationships.

From a development perspective, it is important to hang around with like-minded people. If you are a writer, you might want to develop relationships with other writers, especially those who will push you to be better and grow your skills. If you want to be successful, hang out with successful people. The old birds of a feather flock together; that's a concept that still applies. And the opposite also applies; watch out for negative-energy vampires who suck the life and energy out of you—you know, those who are just plain exhausting to be around. I learned that it's easier to be a positive, optimistic person if you spend time with positive, optimistic people.

You cannot do business without the ability to develop relationships. Having good people skills is necessary unless you drive a truck across the country. I've always joked about the *Top Gun* movie scene in which Maverick and Goose have just been chewed out for doing the unauthorized flyby of the tower and Goose asks Maverick about the name of that trucking company since he'll be looking for a job soon due the stunt Maverick had just pulled. I often think about that scene when it's been a tough people day. And that's saying a lot for me, a highly extroverted person. We all have those moments when we need some alone time to recharge our people batteries.

Growing relationships takes work, time, and intentionality. I've always tried to enjoy getting to know those I have worked with and those I have done business with. Not everyone is as open as I am, but I like to ask questions and learn about people on a basic level. If I am doing a good job of listening, I can learn how others like to operate and how they get energized. At the same time, they can get to know me.

Some relationships take off quickly while others take years to develop, but they all can potentially play a role in my success career-wise. This leadership principle can apply to my personal relationships as well. Do my family members feel valued and listened to when we spend time together? The same question applies to my friends. Think about the four circles in that CCL program I mentioned; if I'm not taking time to develop relationships and I'm all business, my career circle might be overpowering my family and community circles, and I may become a one-trick pony.

John Maxwell talks about relationships on level 2 in his book *The Five Levels of Leadership* (Maxwell 2011). We have all known excellent producers who just left people in their wakes as they motored to their goals. These are folks who tend to be focused on their number one—themselves. I believe these folks are toxic. Yes, they will provide some or many short-term victories, but in the long run, they could destroy your company or business. Developing good relationships is a difference maker in life and in business.

I have the pleasure of working with someone who lives principle 2 each day at the office. He is a magnet for attracting high-performing individuals he then pushes to be the best version of themselves they can be, and they love him. He takes the time to get to know his people as employees and as individuals. He sets the expectations for "meets and exceeds performance" and then holds them accountable for delivering results. He's not easy on them, but the foundation he has poured into them by the relationship building he does creates a strong trust basis for him to push them. He pushes them hard, and they respond well because they believe he has their best interests at heart.

Principle 3—Deliver results.

You can have great relationships in business and life, but if you don't land any planes as I like to say, you won't have a job or long-term success in your career. You have to execute the plan you have been handed or you have developed and drive results. Many times, this is tied to persistency, the ability to hang in there.

In her book *Grit*, Angela Duckworth talks about passion and perseverance (Duckworth 2016). Tying what you do with your passions helps make hanging in there a little more bearable, but it still takes discipline to make it all work. I took a job with a boutique company in Irvine, California. The owner asked me to do something I had never done before—ramp up an introducing broker-dealer, or small securities firm. I had been a stockbroker and then turned into a Credit Union Service Organization (CUSO) executive with a love for the securities industry. I was obsessed with process improvement, so when this business owner called me to offer me this job, I thought, *I could help create a company that does things differently than the other banks, credit unions, and brokerage firms out there.* I thought we could try to improve the customer experience (deliver results) by providing more-personalized service (develop relationships) and making the brokerage business's bureaucracy less burdensome.

This was an awesome opportunity to create something from the ground up, and I was handed a $1 million salary budget to hire the best and brightest in the business and get this operation up and running. I had exactly zero hours of expertise running a broker-dealer, but I had a chance to try something new, hire an awesome staff of difference makers, and get from zero income to profitability within three years.

This endeavor involved developing a strategic plan, a marketing plan, an operations plan, and a people and staffing plan. It was a fantastic opportunity, and I needed to call on some high-level producers with whom I had developed relationships over the years to take a chance and join a brand-new company (or more accurately a new division of an existing company) with no clients, no operating procedures, and no income and become profitable within thirty-six months. Wow! What a rush!

This was another risk I was taking with my career. I had Kim giving me the support I needed after another woulda coulda shoulda chat, yet when I look back at the leadership bet I made when I accepted the Sharonview CEO job, I couldn't help but think about the risks involved with that and other moves I had made. You can call it accepting challenges or making bold moves, but risk is part of the package when you change jobs. Will you be successful? Looking back, was this the right move for your family? It's so important to figure out what makes you tick and what's important to you. I was passionate about helping people and about leadership. Those two key passions were then linked to my Jim Rohn idea of working harder on Bill than I did on my job. That has propelled me, with Kim's support and God's grace, to where I am today.

It was at this little broker-dealer that I truly felt the pressure of the doubting Thomases who all thought this was a bad idea, including a few folks at the parent company! I adopted a theme song during the rough period that first year, "Keep Pushin'" by REO Speedwagon. I would belt out the chorus on my drive to work and gather some confidence about the mission I was on with my team. These people were counting on me, and I didn't want to let them down.

In the first twenty-one months of the business, we drew twenty-one clients away from our chief competitor by delivering better, more-personal service, and we became profitable by month twenty-two! That was a total team effort, and we probably should have celebrated it more than we did. I remembered the countless times I'd been tempted to throw in the towel because the odds seemed insurmountable, but I didn't. I had a feeling that we could make it one client at a time. It was great to see the momentum start to kick in as we began to capture new business. The Stockdale paradox was alive and well at the little broker-dealer that could. In his book *Good to Great,* Jim Collins describes the Stockdale paradox: confronting the brutal facts of the situation you find yourself in but holding onto an unwavering belief that you'll end up successful (Collins 2001).

To add some reality to this broker-dealer story, this is where I made a $1 million mistake but kept my job and lived to tell about it. I was the lead on a project involving some developers to create a client relationship management system. We kept hitting snags; the costs for developing the software kept creeping up. I had to ask repeatedly for a little more money to be spent on development of this or that—highly technical terms for this former stockbroker. I kept the owner up to speed, but we never delivered a working finished product. At the end of the day, I had to be the guy to pull the plug on the project after having spent almost $1 million on it. It was a bad day for me. The owner, whom I had known for over ten years, was not happy, but he decided that this was a great learning experience for us and especially for me.

I have taken with me to this day the grace and support he showed me. The more I've thought about this entrepreneur's act of forgiveness, the more I come back to his attitude of appreciating the wins and learning from any losses. I have adopted the Progress, not Perfection mantra at Sharonview, and it was this situation that helped create this mindset concerning mistakes and grace; a lot of the latter goes a long way when the former happens. And there is no way your team will innovate without your setting the tone about how mistakes will be handled. (See postmortems in principle 10 for more details.)

Relationships and results work together, almost like the scales of justice or a fulcrum; you need to balance both to be successful in business because overweighting in one area or another will provide mixed results. Too much focus on relationships will mean you're the nicest guy or girl in the office but with no visible means of delivering any value to the business or the clients. Too much focus on just winning means you're the jerk who's no fun to be around. You can deliver the goods, but you'll have no one to celebrate with at the victory party.

There are varying degrees of both success factors, but a healthy balance will provide maximum results. See principle 9—Surround yourself with the best people. This involves building relationships. Also see principle 7—Be disciplined. You need to execute plans, and it takes discipline and processes to persevere.

Principle 4—Have a written plan.

I got hung up early in my leadership journey trying to find a formula for success as a leader. I searched for premixed methods, formats, checklists, and tools that would just spell it out for me to follow and *ta da!* I'd be a leader. At age thirty-one, after searching for over two years, I realized that a prepackaged leadership list didn't exist, at least not one that fit me. So I began building out my leadership plan, and I'm still adding to it today, some twenty-nine years later. It's a living, breathing document that I cut into pages and tape in my journal. I make handwritten changes, notes, additions, and deletions during the year to my plan in my journal and update the Excel document[3] to reflect what I consider to be my latest and greatest thinking.

Here are a couple of thoughts for your plan.

1. Pick a tool that will work for you. Excel, Word, Good Reader, OneNote, Pages, Numbers … You get the point. The key is to start capturing your ideas and concepts. What can you use easily so you can have the plan in front of you consistently? Whom will you share the plan with to hold you accountable? Who are the like-minded individuals in your life with whom you want to be open and honest and will help you become the best version of you that you can be?
2. Don't worry if your plan isn't perfect; it will never be perfect. If there were a perfect plan, someone would have bottled it and would be selling it. It has to work for you, and these types of plans are messy. Things change. Circumstances change. Life happens. You need to be flexible and adaptable yet know where you're going. The plan is all about direction—where are you ultimately heading? My mantra, Progress, not Perfection, for Sharonview was the idea that I wanted to ensure that we as a company would embrace moving fast. While we will never practice on our members, we will move forward in a way to challenge ourselves to bring products and services to the marketplace quickly.

---

[3] Go to www.theleadershipbet.com.

We also have used this mantra to describe the servant leadership aspect of forgiveness, providing some grace to staff members and work through how to handle mistakes and failure. Typically, banking errors don't kill anyone or anything; most if not all such mistakes are reversible. With that in mind, we try to do autopsies without casting blame; we figure out what happened and then make sure the member issue is fixed first. Then we try to learn from our mistakes. This attitude goes a long way with folks being more willing to try new things. We want to be a learning and growing company, and people need to know that we will forgive mistakes when best efforts are being put forward.

3. This plan is not just about leadership; it's about my life. Because I am a whole person and not just a leader, my plan addresses all aspects of my life. I am a husband, a father, a grandfather, a son, a brother, a friend … I play many roles day in and day out, and my plan touches all these areas of my life. My plan consists of the following areas (tabs in my Excel workbook).

   a. Individual Development
   b. Activities—Daily, Weekly, Monthly, Quarterly, Semiannually, and Annually
   c. Books to Read
   d. Health Tracker
   e. Workout Schedule
   f. Annual Goals
   g. Purpose Statement
   h. One- to Ten-year Goals

i. Finance Plan (Including my retirement action plan; this is separate from my full-blown financial plan I have set up with an investment professional.)
j. Travel Plan
k. Learning Plan (I call this my table stakes to play the game and What have I learned? area.) Here, I capture great books, sermons, and coaching moments I can easily refer to anytime.

This plan is issued every January and then updated in my journal and eventually my Excel workbook.

I am surprised by how many people I meet who don't have written plans. They don't have to be fancy or long and drawn out, but they need to be written down so people can map their progress, know where they've been, and more important, tell them the direction they're heading.

I have a running joke with my friends and family; when big decisions are being made in the Partin house, I ask God for a burning arrow in the front yard that will point in the direction He wants us to move. He has never actually placed an arrow there, but He has provided clues, people, and circumstances that made evident what direction He wanted us to move in.

Principle 5—Use an idea catcher—a journal.

I use a leather-bound journal full of lined 6" by 9" pages only– that's it. As you read above, I cut out my life plan and create pages in the front of my journal that allow me to track my progress toward my goals. I then update the pages that have been taped in my journal during the year.

When I was in my thirties, I'd tried journaling, but it never stuck; I just never saw the value then. But when I went to work for my mentor at Disney's credit union, he gave me a journal and encouraged me to use it. Just like my written plan, it's mine, and I get to determine how and what goes into it. I had to get comfortable with it getting messy sometimes. It's not perfect, but it's now a big part of how I capture ideas, gather and give feedback to my team, and record my weight Monday through Friday and the number of hours of sleep I get each night. It also houses my daily prayer list. I use two pages per month for these items.

I also collect nice emails or cards people sent me, and I add photos or articles at times. I'm a quick typist, but there's something about using a nice pen to write down ideas, make notes, and just doodle at times. I try to carry it with me everywhere I go at work. I'm starting to take it to church to grab sermon notes instead of using my notes app on my phone.

I'll share a few examples of ways I use my journal today. I'm a big fan of giving and getting feedback. At Sharonview, we use the SBI model I learned at the Center for Creative Leadership in Colorado as follows.

The S stands for situation. Where and when did the feedback moment occur? What meeting, encounter, or circumstance did you find yourself in that created that moment?

The B stands for behavior. This is the difference maker as you are describing the displayed behavior of the people you provided feedback to. What were they saying or doing that caught your attention?

The I is what impact the behavior had on you and how it made you feel.

My wife likes to say that feelings aren't good or bad, that they're just feelings. If nothing else, this model stays away from pronouncing judgment. If I felt great or uncomfortable, those are my calls, and they don't tell the recipient if this was good or bad;

it's just how I felt at the moment of the behavior they displayed. It's a judgment-free zone. And I don't get to tell the recipient how other people felt because I don't know how any others felt.

I capture SBI or what I call general feedback moments/high fives in meetings, informal gatherings, one-on-one interactions, and almost anywhere people gather to work with each other. I write down the situation, the behavior I witnessed, and how I felt about it, or I jot down the situation and some general feedback to share with the individual. Then I try to get to that individual in a timely manner to share the feedback. Our feedback target ratio is 4:1 positive to constructive feedback. (See principle 8 for more details.)

I also write down ideas in my journal and start vetting them. This gives me a chance to try out different ways to attack a problem or situation before I go public. I've scratched out organizational charts and jotted down who would be doing what. We launched a companywide initiative that started in my journal after I had attended several conferences and crafted the beginning of what is now our Business Intelligence Team. Our Operational Excellence initiative started in my journal as well. After that, I'd start whiteboarding with my executive team members individually or as a group to taxi-test the ideas. We would then begin refining them and seeing if they had legs. It's another process I have used to create innovation.

My journal has become an invaluable partner to me over the last fifteen years. You may not be a leather-bound journal kind of person, but I would encourage you to use something to capture your ideas, thoughts, prayer needs, reminders, and so on. If you're electronically inclined, Notes or OneNote work too. Just don't miss the chance to drive your influence up by working smartly, and do not rely on your memory to capture your ideas.

Principle 6—Write down your goals.

Some great writers have captured great ways to do this, including Dan Pink, Jim Rohn, David Allen, and more recently, Angela Duckworth, who wrote *Grit*. I've listed a number of books in the reference section in the back of this book. Many of these authors and their books are among my favorites. Several of them have researched the power of written goals.

Writing down my goals has worked for me and my family. I wrote my first goal list when I was twenty, in 1980. I don't remember why I did it, but I remember how slashing things off my Dad's Saturday chore list created the process-driven dude you're reading about today. It may have started there, but I remember feeling the need to get some things down on paper that I wanted to accomplish, remember, and be reminded of; thus started an annual ritual. I had some constant things on my goal lists, including becoming a stronger Christian, increasing my Bible reading, my school goal of graduating, or my job goals, including roles and positions as well as salary aspirations and career hopes.

As my list of goals grew, I started to categorize them into ongoing, one-year, three-year, five-year, and ten-year goals in my spiritual, health, financial, family, personal, career, and travel aspects of my life.

I use this master goal list to set up my annual goals in my journal with my personal purpose statement. As I mentioned earlier, this is a living document that I make changes to during the year. It's not always pretty, but it's functional, and it works for me. It also forces me to think about how and with whom I want to spend my time.

Sometimes, it's more important to know what to say no to so you can use the finite amount of time you have doing the things that matter most to you. Without a road map, how do you know where you are going and how you are making progress in getting there? I'm not interested in letting life just happen to me; I like to be in control to the greatest extent possible knowing there is a lot I cannot control. One of the best goals write-ups I've come across is in Jim Rohn's *Seven Strategies of Wealth & Happiness* book (Rohn 1996).

Setting goals for whatever you are passionate about is extremely powerful. If you figure out your why, it will drive your what and more important develop your who (i.e. who you are).

Principle 7—Be disciplined.

This is such an important principle even though it sounds so negative. The truth is that without discipline or more to the point disciplines, you may just end up wandering through life without really experiencing it. Jim Rohn talks about how a few simple, positive choices or disciplines repeated daily can create the habits you need to become successful.

He uses the example of eating an apple every day. I'm not sure that doing that will keep the doctor away, but think about how disciplining yourself to grab an apple rather than some candy or chips could lead to better eating habits (Rohn 1996). Making better eating choices can lead to you feeling better and perhaps looking better weight-wise.

Deciding to start walking is another discipline that can be easily started. You can park a little farther from the office and walk. You can take the stairs instead of the elevator (depending on what floor you work on—don't go crazy with this one.) This could lead to your walking your first 5k. The opposite can be true on the negative side of the equation; simple, daily bad choices could impact your health, weight, and so on.

Here's where my goal list and journal come together to create some good habits. As silly as this may sound, I used to crack my knuckles all the time. Nervous habit or just a plain habit, Kim let me know on many occasions that I needed to stop the knuckle cracking or my hands might look like the Hulk's hands when I got older. I decided I would try to stop, so I wrote down on my health goals sheet, "Stop cracking knuckles," and I reviewed that sheet often. Just that simple reminder in my journal got me paying more attention to when I cracked my knuckles or when I felt I wanted to, and I eventually quit doing that. Discipline in the dictionary is described as an activity, exercise, or regimen that develops or improves a skill. I guess you could say I was developing the skill not to crack my knuckles. I keep that one on my health goals just to remind myself about taking care of my hands.

As mentioned, my number-one leadership guiding principle is working harder on yourself than you do on your job, and that ties right in with being disciplined. Rohn talks about the major key to a better future—you! (Rohn 1996). You have to work on you and you alone because you can't change others or things around you because you aren't in control of them, but you are in control of you. "For things to change for you, you have got to change" is what I call a Rohnism. Where discipline fits in here is that you need to make yourself do the necessary things to change the direction of your life. Commit positive acts such as reading, studying, eating the right foods, exercising, and others. Start small, and build up to doing more and more positive acts. This takes self-motivation. This takes hanging out with the right people, so find yourself some right people.

I'm disciplined when it comes to even starting my day. I connect with God by praying during my forty-minute drive to the office. I spend some quiet time when I arrive at the office reading a devotional or the Bible and thinking about what I just read. And on three or four mornings, I try to exercise. One or two mornings, I head to the YMCA and play racquetball with a friend, who usually wipes the court with me, but it's a great workout. I'll hit the treadmill, tread climber, or stationary bike the other two days. It's a great way to kick-start my day, and the exercise time and the God time gets me in a great frame of mind to take on my day.

Principle 8—Give and gather feedback all the time.

For me to be the best version of Bill I can be, I need help understanding my impact on those around me. By working on being self-aware, I can know where I need to turn things up and just as important where to turn things down. I have been a fan of feedback throughout my career. I have always challenged myself to be vulnerable and open enough to listen to feedback. Be sure to thank your feedback providers and decide if and how to use the feedback. I heard years ago that feedback was a gift, and I love that way of viewing it. It's my choice to use or discard the gift.

The SBI model I described earlier is the most effective way to give and receive feedback; it takes judgment out of the equation if done properly. Also, the premise with SBI is that you work toward pouring more positive feedback moments into a person so that when you deliver a correcting piece of feedback, you can be heard. This notion of feedback ties in with working harder on yourself than you do on your job. I can't get better unless I understand how I am being perceived and impacting others.

Feedback also can be given generally, but it's not as impactful. Still, my goal as a leader is to create an environment in which feedback is the norm. Normally when you hear "I need to give you some feedback," most people immediately head to the negative side of the room. Feedback in general has been given a bad rap. We have tried to turn that negative feeling around by creating an environment in which people want feedback. If the environment is set up well, it'll be one in which people give feedback and welcome receiving it. The goal is everyone around you at work is involved taking their game to the next level. As you practice your craft, wouldn't it be great to get encouragement along the way?

As mentioned, CCL recommends based on research that we should strive for a 4:1 ratio of positive to correcting feedback to provide high-quality experiential growth. I have read additional research that the ratio should be 9:1 for a family. Telling my wife, children, or grandchildren what they specifically did and how it impacted me is an area I need to work on more.

Feedback helps address my blind spots. A concept was shared with me called the Johari Window. That window has four quadrants: areas I self-disclose about myself, areas about myself I'm blind to, areas I choose not to disclose about myself, and areas that are unknown to me. The feedback focus helps me understand the blind spots I have in how I am perceived by others and the impact I'm having. Without getting feedback, I'll never know how my behavior is being received. That's another reason I love the SBI model; how I impact someone else is not a matter of right or wrong; the feelings my behavior invokes in others are theirs and theirs alone. Armed with that feedback, I then get to choose to change my behavior or not. Again, feedback is the gift I can choose how to use.

Also, I ask for feedback. If I'm attempting to land some planes regarding a big point I need to make in a meeting or in a talk, I plant one of my feedback partners (find a couple of these folks who will give it to you straight regardless of your position in the organization) in the room and ask them to watch and listen for the points I'm trying to drive home. That allows me to gauge how effectively I delivered my message and understand my impact on my feedback partner via SBI. I am intentional on this personal development area. Surround yourself with the best people, those who will tell you the unvarnished truth as Nathan did for King David. I call such people in my life my Nathans.

Two other methods of getting feedback involve two tools I've used successfully. One is the Skip Level Feedback model.[4] I've always joked that my direct reports can tell me about how great they are, but it's another thing to skip over them and ask their people how they're doing. We have adapted the model that the Center for Creative Leadership uses for leadership. This model looks at competencies including collaboration, leadership, and self-awareness. We score each section and offer participants who are providing the feedback a chance to provide comments and examples for the recipient to help enrich the process. A score is great, but tangible facts on how I, the leader, am affecting those I work with are invaluable helps to me to become a better version of me.

Over the last several years, we have incorporated the skip level with our 360-degree process in evaluating leaders and especially those who are up for promotions. It's become a great tool as we do full-calibration sessions with the executive leadership team in weighing all aspects of peoples' capabilities and not just taking the word of their leaders that they are having the type of impact we need in our organization.

Second, we employ the tried and tested Start, Stop and Continue concept.[5] I used this format when I first arrived at Sharonview to get a feeling for what was working and what was

---

[4] See www.theleadershipbet.com.

[5] See www.theleadershipbet.com.

broken. The questions are all free-form and open-ended: What should we start doing that we currently do not do? What should we stop doing that we are currently doing? What should we continue doing that is a current practice today? You'll be surprised what you will learn. I do these anonymously to ensure people feel free to tell me what's on their minds. I look for trends and areas that are consistently mentioned more than one or two comments here and there. I couple this feedback with some visits to the departments and to every branch to get a sense of how things are really going regardless of the written responses. Such in-person visits and the Start, Stop, and Continue method are what helped me determine what we needed to work on first.

Principle 9—Surround yourself with the best people.

John Maxwell calls this the Law of the Inner Circle. In Maxwell's *Leadership Bible*, he created an acronym from the words *inner circle* to help describe what it means to create an inner circle. The words are *influence, network, nurture, empower, resourceful, character driven, intuitive, responsible, competent, loyal,* and *energetic* (Maxwell 2014). I'll let you tie your own definitions to each letter, but people with these characteristics can be great members of a team.

Jim Collins, author of *Good to Great*, says it best—First who then what. I have always believed that you need to surround yourself with people who are smarter, more articulate, and better looking than yourself. Well, that last one's a stretch, but you get my point. I don't want any yes people on my team; I want people who will challenge me and others professionally and come up with a better solution to a problem or a better product than the one first put on the table. This principle means everyone has the right and in fact the obligation to share his or her thoughts on the subject being discussed. One of our board members put it best—"If we all thought the same, I wouldn't need you on the team." Be a contributor, a challenger, a contrarian—and do all those things in a way that creates the best version of whatever you are working on.

Here are two stories about how I saw this principle in action. One involves hiring a high powered, well-tenured executive on my team. And you know the drill ... The new guy needs to ease into our executive team meetings slowly and take the temperature of the room before jumping in with both feet. He needs to wait his turn. Well, he did no such thing. He immediately weighed in on a very meaty subject, and he didn't agree with the group. He eloquently argued a position that was based on his big-shop experience, and it sucked the air out of the room for a minute before the discussion continued. I was very impressed, and his ideas ultimately led us to a great decision. This non-yes person made a huge impression on the rest of the team that day too.

My second story involves a coach my son had in football. My son decided in seventh grade that he wanted to play Junior All American (JAA) football. This is tackle football, and we loved it because Pop Warner played on Sundays, which would have totally disrupted our church lives, and JAA played on Saturdays. Our son had just finished playing flag football and had fallen in love with football. He was fast, he loved to carry the ball, and he had some natural talent for the game. He then was blessed to play for a JAA coach whom I still admire. I can't remember his name, but I do remember how he took a bunch of individual performers and created a team. He was the best coach for my son I had ever seen at that level; he put each player in a position that might not have been that player's preferred role, but he pulled the best out of each player and made this group of guys a team. It was a thing of beauty. The coach took what he was dealt talent-wise and put them in the best positions for the sake of the team to create the best possible outcomes for these twenty-two young men.

Principle 10—Conduct premortems and postmortems.

I have practiced postmortems for much of my career. Being a huge fan of feedback, I have always looked for what I could learn after a large project or program was completed. What went well? What didn't and why? We would work to catalog the hits and address the misses. I like to call this doing an autopsy without any blame. It's not who missed the mark but what was overlooked that caused the mark to be missed; we could learn from those mistakes rather than repeat them. At Sharonview, the mantra Progress, not Perfection was actually captured as one of our core values, and we decided that this concept would apply to the idea of continually moving forward and the realization that we wouldn't always execute perfectly individually or as a company but that we could learn from our successes and failures alike as individuals and as a company.

Premortems was a new concept I picked up at a Stanford University Executive Education session I attended several years ago. The idea hit me that we needed to adopt this concept and lay it against our postmortems. What a great set of bookends to help us learn and grow. Here's basically how the process works; it's been Partinized as I call it. For a project to be wildly successful however that is defined eighteen months from now, what needs to be true or needs to happen today to ensure success? We decided to focus just on the positive attributes of the equation because for the most part, the negative attributes were most often just the opposite of the positive attributes. For example, for us to successfully launch Member Business Lending and for it to be wildly successful eighteen months from now, we decided we had to

1. dedicate time, training, and resources for our retail delivery team,
2. dedicate time, training, and resources for our member services operations team,
3. determine the types of businesses we will and won't serve, and
4. determine the geographic markets we will and won't serve.

We created a one- to two-page document that became our bible as we work our way through the project. If we started to veer off course, we could come back to true north by reviewing our premortem. This practice has served us well and helps us get our best thinking out on the table early in a new process, product, or procedure. We have actually built this concept into our operational excellence process today, where the vetting of an idea is looked at through the long-term success lens.

Principle 11—Be a servant leader.

James C. Hunter's book *The Servant* (Hunter 1998) changed my perspective on a belief I'd had for years about showing those who worked for me that I cared about them, their families, their interests, and what was important to them. It's all about developing relationships with those you work with so you can help them play to their strengths and become the best version of themselves they can become.

I spoke earlier about the two leadership success factors—relationships and results. Being a servant leader is all about the relationship part—putting others first, forgiving others, showing them kindness, being helpful, and being patient. Here was the difference maker for me—love, as in love the verb. In Hunter's book, he quotes Vince Lombardi – "I don't necessarily have to like my players and associates, but as their leader, I must love them. Love is loyalty, love is teamwork, love respects the dignity of the individual. This is the true strength of any organization." Lombardi's quote is about love the verb, not love the feeling. Love was what I wanted to convey to my teams. It's a radical thought in today's nonconfrontational world. Love the verb denotes actions, not feelings. The list above is about action.

I have challenged my leaders to love their teams, and I have challenged everyone in the entire organization to love each other and our members. We demonstrate love by how we treat each other and how we treat our members. The funny thing is that we have a core value about building relationships through genuine care and concern. We call that the Wow! I call that love.

Think about this principle and principle 1. The combination of being a servant leader and working on becoming the best version of you that you can be—that's a powerful combination that can change your perspective. I came to this realization at age thirty-six, when I had just landed a huge job at a huge credit union in Manhattan Beach, California. I finally had the title, the office (complete with the former CEO's gold-inlaid furniture), a couch, and a refrigerator. I had arrived. I was the man! And I was miserable within three months of landing that big job. I realized that the stuff wasn't what I was after. The chance to develop my people and myself and work on getting better and better at this leadership thing was what got me going and kept me going.

Building up people, encouraging them, helping them find their wheelhouse, and then turning them loose to perform or get results tied to our strategy was exhilarating. Within nine or ten months after I took that job, I realized what I wanted to do for the rest of my career— develop high-performing teams of people who enjoyed working hard, having fun, and knocking the lights out of our strategic targets for the benefit of our members or customers.

I had the opportunity through our church to lead a group of young men through a twelve-month study about becoming better men, better husbands, and better followers of God. I considered myself the perfect guy to lead this group because of all the imperfect things I'd done over the years that I had learned from and continue to learn from to this day.

We read a book a month and spent time in small groups and as a large group sharing life and our challenges as men and developing a deeper understanding of God's plans for our lives. It was a tremendous honor and challenge to lead this group. We practiced love, the verb. Many of those relationships continue today, and it's my pleasure to watch these young men grow in their faith and in their relationships with their wives and children. They're working on being servant leaders and becoming the best versions of themselves they can become together.

Patrick Lencioni wrote *The Ideal Team Player*, mandatory reading for every leader at Sharonview. It describes three attributes we look for in Sharonview's employees and those we're considering hiring. First, are they humble? Do they have servants' hearts? Second, are they hungry? Are they striving to learn and improve themselves, or as I like to think about it, are they becoming the best version of themselves they can become? Third, are they smart? Not book smart but people smart? Can they work in teams and collaborate with others to get things done? (Lencioni 2016). These attributes are embedded in our culture, and they help support who we are and how we do things. They also line up well with our core values.

- We build relationships through genuine care and concern.
- Employees are the cornerstone of our success.
- Work-life balance is how we live.
- Open and honest communication is what we do.
- We will grow and improve from our mistakes – "progress, not perfection".

Principle 12—Have fun!

Life is too short not to do what you enjoy doing. How many of you know people who are just plain miserable in their jobs? People who dread going to work? Unfortunately, if you spend any amount of time with them, that subject always surfaces. As I said earlier, when you find your why, it will connect you to your what, what you should be doing. The ideal scenario is that you love what you do and you do what you love; when you're in that zone or flow, life is good!

Our daughter and son-in-law practice this principle every day. They can turn an ordinary drive somewhere into an adventure, and once they stop the car, the adventure continues. I love their attitude, and it's not about spending a ton of money; it's about being in the moment and seeing things others just pass by. I relate this principle to my favorite movie, *Top Gun*. Okay, don't judge. During the movie, Goose is killed, and Maverick can't make the comeback to flying again at the level he was capable of. He's sitting in a bar with a ticket to nowhere. His girlfriend, callsign Charlie, comes in to talk with him. She tells him that he won't be happy unless he's going Mach 2 with his hair on fire. I love that line; it went into my personal purpose statement. I want to live life Mach 2 with my hair on fire. With my haircut, that fire wouldn't last long, but you get the point. I want to go full tilt and have fun in everything I do—work, play, etc., with friends, family, and coworkers. Do what you love and love what you do.

What do you do when you're not having fun? The good news here is that you're the one in control of you. How are you handling the non-fun times? You know they will come. This ties in with creating a process and having the discipline to follow it through thick and thin, the fun times and not-so-fun times. It's easier to work through the not-so-fun times when you're connected to something you're passionate about and love doing.

CHAPTER 8
GOD

If you aren't a big believer in God or don't feel there is a God, you may want to skip this chapter. I'm a big fan of God, and I've continued to try to serve Him and listen to Him even though my God hearing is poor. I'm thankful that He's patient, all powerful, and present in my life. He's the reason we're in North Carolina today.

I heard a great sermon recently that talked about how God is ready to bless you, but you have to commit (something about "Seek ye first ..."). You must make the first move, listening to God. The book of Hebrews talks about learning from God and trusting Him to show up after He has told you where He wants you and what He wants you to be doing; the blessing follows the commitment. This was completely true in our case. Remember the joke with my family and friends about looking for the burning arrow in the yard after praying for God to show us the way? "What do you want me, us, to do, Lord? Which way do you want us to go? Was Sharonview the place you wanted us? What do you want us to do once we get there?" We had a ton of questions, but we felt God was steering us east. We were not at all sure why, but we felt this was the right call. (Maybe me more than Kim originally.) We had no idea how He would use us there, but we ventured out on faith and felt He would make His ways clear to us. And did He ever confirm our decision, right out of the gate.

In his book *Whisper*, Mark Batterson describes five tests you can apply to God-sized dreams and the will of God. Test 1 is the goose bump test; he writes that your heart will skip a beat as you consider a monumental task in front of you. Test 2 is the peace test. He talks about having a holy confidence against all odds versus being scared out of your wits. Test 3 is the wise counsel test. We are to seek wise counsel. Test 4 is the crazy test. Check that one as we described what we had decided to do to our friends and family. Test 5 is the released-from and called-to test. I believe we experienced several of these tests just before and right after we made the decision to try this Sharonview thing (Batterson 2017).

Once we said yes and talked to our son and daughter about this crazy move, God started knocking over some big dominoes. Here are several examples that we were on His path. After we decided to take the job, we put our house on the market; that was at the end of summer 2013 in LA. The real estate market was a little soft, so we priced our house to move, but then God got involved; within three days, we had three offers over full price—Crazy!

Second, we had an idea of where we wanted to move to in the Charlotte area, but the original thought I had due to the horrible drive I'd endured for the last several years at Disney was to buy a place a couple of miles from the office. *Perfect!* I thought, but Kim had different thoughts. We love to water ski, and there was a lake semi-close to my new office. For years, we had been driving five and a half hours to the family-friendly Lake San Antonio in Monterey County to escape the crowds on the lakes near LA, so being able to get to the lake in twenty or thirty minutes appealed to me. Kim and I were pros at launching boats after having done so many times over twenty-three years. I'd back the trailer into the water, and she would jump in and pull the boat off the trailer. We were fast at it. I'd be digressing if I even mentioned that one of our favorite pastimes was watching people trying to launch their boats or jet skis.

The Leadership Bet

I guess we were thinking too small there too. God plopped us down in a great neighborhood on Lake Wylie with a boat dock complete with a lift, so no more launching our boat from a ramp. And He didn't stop there—we paid $3,000 less than what we'd sold our LA home for, and it had twice the space and over half an acre of property—real land, something I joked about earlier. We owned a little now. No fences, great neighbors—something we thought we would not experience again based on how great our neighbors were in So Cal at our last home. And don't tell anyone this, but the cost of living is half of what we were used to in LA. Well, maybe not half … but close to it.

I learned why they called South Carolina part of the Bible Belt. God was openly talked about, and prayers were said at sporting events, political events, work events … It was awesome. Asking someone if you could pray for them is not a federal offense here, and I love that!

I walked into Sharonview and knew early on that I was in over my head. First, nothing was broken for me to fix. I mean nothing glaring. The numbers were solid, the senior management team seemed solid, and the place seemed comfortable. I felt it was a good, strong organization. They had a focus on leadership development, but it was in its infancy stage. The same was true with the project management office; it was in place but had no real legs.

I wasn't sure where to start, but I knew I needed to lay all my questions, concerns, and worries at the foot of the cross and ask God for help. I went into complete dependency mode, which is not an area I like to be in. But He had some lessons for me to learn, and I started to work on my hearing Him with a ton of prayer and spending quiet time each morning at the office after driving for forty minutes praying on the way to work.

That prayer time, that quiet time five days a week really sharpened my listening skills, and I have felt the Holy Spirit nudge me regarding problems, opportunities, and personnel issues over the last six years. I take God into every meeting, and sometimes, I write in my journal LBWM—Lord be with me. He's in my premeeting work, and we talk after many meetings. I find myself doing a football quarterback pose at times after He's shown up; I stop, look at the ceiling, and point up thanking Him for being with me in that meeting, in the boardroom, or after a tough personnel meeting. Of course I do this in the privacy of my office or while walking down a hallway with no one around to see a crazy CEO pointing to the sky, but here's the truth—He shows up again and again.

I also write in my journal TYL—Thank you, Lord—when I sense Him showing up. It's here I need to give Him the glory He deserves. God has been faithful (I wish I could say the same) 100 percent of the time! I thought about just slipping in a reference here and there in this book about Him, but I just couldn't limit it to that. He's been too big, too present, and too evident to leave Him out of my story. It's because of Him I have a story anyway!

Principle 13—Believe.

The Stockdale paradox mentioned earlier is about confronting the brutal facts of the situation you find yourself in but nonetheless holding onto the unwavering belief that you will be successful. When I think about believing in what I'm doing, I first must be grounded in the fact that I'm doing what I love to do and hopefully having fun doing it. That entails ensuring I am involved in something that is worthwhile and bigger than me. That's really what landed me in credit union land in the first place; I loved the business model of a credit union being not-for-profit and owned by its members.

Belief for me also means that there is a God who put me here on this planet for His purpose. My job is to listen carefully to what that purpose is and lean on Him to get it done. It's not the Bill Partin show—it's His show. I talked earlier about the CCL concept that involved a spiritual wrapper of sorts around the four areas of a person's life as they outline it—self, career, family, and community—and the wrapper is different for everyone. My wrapper is God, His Son, and the Holy Spirit. Armed with faith, I believe God is the reason I ended up as the CEO of Sharonview, a job I didn't think I was ready for. God, however, had a different idea and put me in way over my head so I would believe in Him, lean on Him, and depend on Him to be successful.

When I started at Sharonview, the retiring CEO let me in on a couple of secrets. First, he told me that though the board of directors had said he would stick around for as long as I needed him, that wasn't going to happen; he was leaving in two weeks. I started to protest, but he said something that will stick with me forever; I've used it in my leadership playbook since then. He said that until he got out of there, I'd not really be running the place, that people would continue to sneak over to find out what he thought or how he thought this or that should be done. Boy, looking back, I realize he was spot-on.

He also told me that I was going to have an Oh crap! moment or two or three where I would place my head in my hands and ask myself, *What have I gotten myself into?* He nailed that one as well; that happened several times in the first year of my CEOship. But my belief in God and the ability He had given me kept me going.

Toby Mac sings the song "Beyond Me." I can totally relate to it because our move to the Carolinas got me on my knees and asking daily for His help. The lyrics[6] go like this.

    Call it a reason to retreat
I got some dreams that are bigger than me
I might be outmatched outsized the underdog in the fight of my life
Is it so crazy to believe
    That you gave me the stars put them out of my reach
Call me to waters a little too deep
Oh I've never been so aware of my need
You keep on making me see
It's way beyond me
It's way beyond me
Yeah it's out of my league
It's way beyond me
It's way beyond me
It's way beyond
    Anything that I got the strength to do
In over my head keeps me countin' on you
I'm leaving the sweet spot sure shot tradin' it all for the plans you got
Is it so crazy to believe
    That you gave me the stars put them out of my reach
Call me to waters a little too deep
Oh I've never been so aware of my need
You keep on making me see
It's way beyond me
It's way beyond me

---

[6] See acknowledgement page for permission

Yeah it's out of my league
It's way beyond me
It's way beyond me
    You take me to the place where I know I need You
Straight to the depths that I can't handle on my own
And Lord I know, I know I need You
So take me to Your great
Take me to Your great unknown
    It's way beyond me, way way beyond me
It's it's way beyond me, way way way beyond me
    Yeah, You gave me the stars, put them out of my reach
Called me to waters just a little too deep
Oh, I've never been so aware of my need
Yeah, you keep on making me see
It's way beyond me (it's way beyond me)
It's way beyond me (it's way beyond me)
Yeah, it's out of my league (it's way beyond me)
It's way beyond me (it's way beyond me)
It's way beyond me (it's way beyond me)
It's way beyond me
    You take me to the place where I know I need You
Straight to the depths that I can't handle on my own (it's way beyond me)
You take me to the place where I know I need You
Oh take me to Your place
Take me to Your great unknown

    That was me when we said yes to Sharonview.

CHAPTER 9
THE LEADERSHIP BET

The leadership bet is not a gamble – it's a calculated risk that everything rises and falls on leadership. The outcomes of our company, the success of our people, the way our customers, or members, or stakeholders feel about us all rests on the focus of delivering great leadership to our team.

When I accepted the CEO role at Sharonview, I decided to place a high premium on leadership with the following thoughts: How do I take a good organization and assemble a strong leadership team to make it a great one? What did that mean, and how would this premium show itself in the day-to-day running of a billion-dollar credit union?

I felt this would need to be attacked on several fronts. First, we needed to create an environment that showed that leadership was important by cranking up the leadership development program that was in place. This program needed a champion besides the head of human resources or what we now call talent management; we needed to take the program to the next level, and I wanted to insert a Center for Creative Leadership approach. I mentioned earlier that I'm a big fan of building on ideas others have tried and tested and not reinventing the wheel; I was more than willing to draft off other successful concepts and ideas and of course Partinizing them—making them my own. I wanted to blend my CCL experience and the leadership work my previous CEO had instituted at the Disney credit union into something that would work for Sharonview. When I arrived, we had a ton of solid managers but not very many leaders or a common leader language; we had an every person for himself or herself mentality; it was silo central.

We started by pulling together a leadership training and coaching team or at least the main facilitator, his first lieutenant, and his fitness and wellness coach. This group was almost the same team we had used at the Disney credit union; I told you I was a big fan of Partinizing great ideas. We invited them to put together an intense five-day program that included several assessments, including Myers-Briggs, Benchmarks 360, Emotional Intelligence, and a FIRO-B assessment along with some physical fitness and dietary work. I decided we needed for the chiefs to go first—the executive leadership team or what we called then the senior management team. We would see how this changed us as a group, and then we'd be able to make some modifications and drive this new leadership development program down through the organization.

That was the beginning of the new Sharonview Leadership Development Program (SLDP), and when I look back, I note that we've traveled a tremendous distance forward in improving the program. I also recall how hard several members of the senior management team fought against some aspects of the program. There were several naysayers regarding the physical exercise portion of the program, which included yoga. Not that any of us looked good at 6:00 in the morning in our yoga outfits, but such feedback let me know how tough it was for people to change and that we had some work to do on the chief level to move forward as a company.

The fighting has been worth it when I look back to see how far we have come as a company. And the leadership bet I placed needed this program to drive up our level of leadership or influence across the organization. We needed a common language.

We needed a common footing on how to deliver and receive feedback. We needed to develop our leadership muscles by reading good books together and incorporating some key concepts into our company if we wanted it and ourselves to grow.

We adopted John Maxwell's *Five Levels of Leadership* as one of our cornerstone books. Patrick Lencioni's *The Ideal Team Player* was also incorporated into our leadership playbook. As the leaders in the organization started figuring out that the tide was rising around leadership, some opted out while some dug in and took their game to a whole new level.

Second, we needed to insert some processes to support my passion for leadership. My belief was that if we created great leaders, we would generate the environment that created and sustained high Net Promoter Scores (Fred Reichheld 2006) and Wow! experiences for our members along with creating a fantastic environment for our teams to work in. This started with our needing to set expectations with my team and then for my team to set expectations with their direct reports right down the line. We could then link our strategy to everyone in the joint and be clear about what we were about and how we needed to help our members.

Goals and Objectives Notebooks and Playbooks[7]

These processes included setting up goals and objectives notebooks, what we call G&Os. These notebooks captured Key Projects, Key Measures, Leadership, and People. We created a version for the staff as well that we call playbooks. The purpose of these documents was twofold: to have conversations at least monthly about results versus our agreed-upon goals and to

---

[7] G&O notebook and playbook examples are available at www.theleadershipbet.com.

outline behaviors we expected at Sharonview. The monthly part and the form for our managers and staffers were new. Prior to my arrival, Sharonview had conducted midyear and year-end performance appraisals. What I found across the organization was that we had managers just checking a box to get this transaction done. Leaders—I mean managers—were not meeting with their staffers to specifically talk about how they were doing versus the expectations that were (that actually hadn't actually been set up to that point) set in the G&O.

I rolled out the G&Os with my direct reports, the senior management team (SMT). I needed to get my team on board before I could get their teams on board, so we started this practice right away. It was bumpy out of the gate, but the SMT started to get the swing of this thing. Here's the beauty of the G&O: once the key projects and key measures for the area were negotiated, the updates were being reported to me or to the employee's direct leader by each SMT member or employee.

The second purpose of the G&O was that it became a self-reporting vehicle. Based on the self-reports being submitted twenty-four hours before we met (and I started off meeting with my direct reports weekly there), I'd review the G&Os and be prepared to ask questions about areas I wanted to focus on for our check-in. I would take notes during the check-in, and the G&O would build during the year based on those notes. This document would become the primary documentation for the midyear and annual performance appraisals. And the check-in meeting became the direct report's meeting quickly, in that the G&O could be reviewed fairly quickly, which left time for whatever the employee wanted to focus on.

The chief experience of our new leadership development program happened within twelve months of my arrival at Sharonview.

The Leadership Bet

I knew we needed to adjust the set of our sails on leadership right away. During that first experience, we had some tough discussions about how things had been done up to that point in the company, and we decided as a group that some things needed to change if we were going to climb to new heights as a company.

Remember that I had not inherited a broken company; in fact, that would have been easier to deal with when it came to fixing what needed fixing. We were trying to work out new rules of engagement to go from good to great. We decided to move away from the old triangulation model of communication where one SMT member would talk to the CEO and expect him to fix an issue he or she was having with someone. Each chief became empowered to go directly to the person he or she needed to talk with to work out any problems. We talked about truly living the SBI feedback model publicly or privately as needed and appropriate.

Being direct, candid, and empathic became how we began to work together. (Today, I would insert the word *love*—the verb. We will love each other enough to tell the truth and help each other become the best versions of ourselves.) We changed the name of our group to the Executive Leadership Team (ELT) to more clearly call out that we were executive leaders rather than managers.

We also established our new group norms, what we called our rules of engagement for the ELT. They included no triangulation; provide direct feedback both positive and constructive, trying to abide by the 4:1 ratio; use data, facts, and figures (what I call DFF) to make decisions; and have fun! The amazing thing about these changes was that the entire staff was watching us learn, grow, and challenge each other to become better at leading, and they were excited about the new ELT. That excitement showed up in our employee engagement scores later that year.

Key projects were projects that a leader and her or his direct report had agreed upon. The projects needed to be key, and they needed to tie in with our overall strategy. We have ebbed and flowed on how many projects worked on the G&O. We'd seen too many but then not enough over the last five years. It's an art rather than a science for sure. These are typically a combination of large, enterprise-wide (i.e. run by the Project Management Office) type of projects along with some department-only projects. The goal was to create short updates that the owners of the G&Os submitted to their leaders to ensure project progress and accountability and get help with bigger projects as needed.

We also worked on the People section that reflected the leader's direct reports. Who was in progression? Were there any voluntary or involuntary terminations? Were there any new hires? It was straightforward human resources stuff. There was also an area dedicated to how leaders were working with their teams on their engagement work from the previous survey, and we added sections about SBI feedback, coaching buddies (we paired up leaders from across the company to help support each other with people coaching, feedback, etc.), and meaningful feedback moments—giving or receiving.

The last original G&O section was Leadership. This was the area in which the leaders would document what they were doing to grow their leadership skills and abilities (e.g., what books were being read, what seminars or webinars had been attended that were more personal development–oriented versus business related, etc.). This was the area where these types of activities were to be captured and shared with their leader. This section morphed into what we now call the individual development plan (IDP).

Individual Development Plans[8]

The individual development plans were based on people's current roles in the company; the leaders would list what each was doing in his or her current role to become better as a leader. Based on other managers' feedback, engagement survey feedback, or our SLDP feedback, a few key items would be selected by the individual completing the self-reporting tool, and monthly updates would be provided.

The next section was what I like to call the "What do you want to be when you grow up?" section. I wanted the employees to dream a little and come up with the next role they wanted to shoot for at Sharonview. People could report, "I want to become the VP of Member Services" even if that position didn't exist at the time.

Jim Rohn talks about the journey being more important than the destination (or in this case the title). He says that it's not what you get in the end but what you become as you travel toward the destination that is the difference maker (Rohn 1996). To that end, I wanted to create a safe place for folks to stretch themselves in search of becoming the best version of themselves. The section became a great topic of conversation during the check-ins, and the leaders would need to be on their toes to ensure they were helping their direct reports stretch and grow.

As the G&O trickled down through the organization over a two-year period, people started noticing something—the accountability level began to rise during that time. You couple the accountability going up with getting serious about providing feedback to each other—peer to peer, leader to staff, and staff

---

[8] Individual development plan samples can be found at www.theleadershipbet.com.

to leader—and look out! It started to break down the silos. It also increased our turnover rate. Sharonview had had a very low turnover rate—2 to 4 percent on average—over the ten years prior to my arrival. As we started working across and down the organization setting clear expectations and measuring to those expectations as well as providing feedback, some people starting opting out and moving on.

These two tools didn't get put into place without some fights. We had an all-out mutiny at the All Leader's Meeting when we rolled out the G&O notebooks and our playbooks from the leaders to the staff, but we answered their questions, dealt with the pushback, and got this program disseminated to the rest of the organization. I am happy to say that with the combination of feedback and work on the G&Os, we are getting ready to take our next step of progress and kill the annual performance appraisal system. I love it when a plan comes together!

Memo of Expectations (MOE)[9]

I decided up front that I wanted to lay out my expectations for my direct reports, the ELT. I was very specific about all aspects of being a solid member of the ELT, so I left nothing to chance in the first version of this document. I called out time frames to return calls, emails, and so on, along with my thoughts about being collaborative and working across the organization. It turned out to be about a five-page document, but we've trimmed it down to one page, over time, and it was embedded with our core values except for this last year. Last year, I wanted to convey that the members of the ELT needed to work not only in their downline

---

[9] MOE samples can be found at www.theleadershipbet.com.

but also across the organization, and I tied the memo to being a level-4 leader as per Maxwell (Maxwell 2011).

In trying to create a feedback culture in which leadership was required to really move our organization, I felt it was important to make sure the expectations were clear, straightforward. That really differed from the playbooks in that there were points I wanted to negotiate with my direct reports and vice versa. I wanted them to own their key projects and key measures so that we could negotiate what ended up in the notebook that was tied to our strategy. This concept helped me drive ownership of corporate goals one employee at a time. Everybody had a piece of our strategic pillars and priorities, and together, we created Wow! moments for our members by being aligned in our aims and goals.

How Do You Know All This Leadership Stuff Works Anyway?

I wrote earlier about relationships and results. Let me share our results as a company over the last six years and even some results from my previous credit union experience at Disney. One of the primary gauges for us as a leadership team is how engaged our staff is. I used to ask the interview question about which group was more important to our credit union—our members or our staff. It was really a trick question because both had very important roles. But I've watched how creating engaged employees over the last fourteen years has been a difference maker for our members, and I became convinced that treating the employees as the cornerstone of our success was key! We have used the Employer's Association (TEA) in the Charlotte area to do our annual employee engagement survey. This survey gives us a ton of great data, including how many employees feel fully engaged, how many feel partially engaged, and how many feel disengaged. Fully engaged means that we as a company are getting the benefit of an employee's discretionary efforts consistently. Partially engaged is where we sometimes get that discretionary effort and other times don't. You can guess what disengaged means—an employee may be trying to undermine the work of the organization.

We've ranged from the high 40 percent range to the high 60 percent range for fully engaged over the last six years. These scores were coupled with scores for the disengaged at 1 percent for five of the six years; the other year, it was at 4 percent. National averages from TEA for professional services organizations average 30 percent to 33 percent for fully engaged and 18 percent for disengaged.

What I really liked about the survey results were the verbatim comments our employees shared. We typically asked two to three questions, including "What do you like about working at Sharonview?" and "What should we consider changing about Sharonview?" We typically receive a ton of great comments on both sides of the ledger. These comments and the corresponding scores were used to help us work to keep doing the things that were working (continue doing) and improve areas we needed to focus on where we saw big trends that needed to be addressed (possibly start and possibly stop doing). Our next stop here is to become the employer of choice for financial institutions in the markets we serve!

We spend a tremendous amount of time working with our staff to develop relationships that would drive great performance. One measure of performance is our financials. From 2014 through 2018, we saw triple and quadruple growth of our key performance measures around asset growth, member growth, loans, and deposit growth. Those results were easy to track. It was tougher to gauge how we were being perceived in the marketplace by our members. Were we delivering exceptional value to our over eighty-eight thousand members in the Carolinas and New Jersey?

One of our industry groups that attempts to measure this member value is Callahan and Associates. They have titled this measurement Return to the Member, ROM. Callahan has developed a scoring model that attempts to determine the value to the membership per credit union on the savings side of the ledger, on the lending side of the ledger, and then on our fees charged for various member services. Each component is then scored, and Callahan totals up all the areas for an overall score. That score can then be used to compare credit unions in terms of how member-friendly they are with the fees and rates they charge their members as well as the rates they pay their members for deposits. It's something we pay a lot of attention to so we can determine if our pricing strategies, our fees-for-services strategies, and our overall member service strategy is winning. Our results have been and continue to be impressive. We have been in the top 5 percent for the last five years of over three hundred credit unions serving in North and South Carolina and New Jersey.

Even with all the changes we instituted in our organization, the team is continuing to create Wow! moments for our members, and we're continuing to receive Net Promoter Scores (NPSs) in the high 80 percent range (currently 88 percent). To put this in perspective, according to the CustomerGauge report for 2018, the average financial services industry NPS score is 46 percent with world class being a score of 70 percent or more. This is a great tribute to the staff who have seen us move from Sharon who to Sharonview by raising the level of awareness in every market we serve.

One of the top accolades we've received as a company came in 2018 when *Forbes* ranked Sharonview the number-one consumer choice credit union in South Carolina (we are headquartered in Indian Land, South Carolina, even though we have branches in North Carolina and New Jersey as well as elsewhere in South Carolina).

Making the leadership bet has paid dividends to the over three hundred employees at Sharonview and therefore for the over eighty-eight thousand (and growing) members who call Sharonview their financial institution.

CHAPTER 10
CLOSING THOUGHTS

Making the leadership bet took years of disciplined practice, a lot of trial and error, and working my plan to put me in a position to work with one of the top two hundred credit unions in the country. And it didn't come without risks. The risk of leaving my home in California. The risk of not being successful as a CEO of a credit union. The risk that Kim might hate the East Coast and not be thrilled about having to start over at a new church and make new friends. Much could have gone wrong. But that same bet mentality that got me ready has seen me through to now. With more to do, I felt it was time to tell the story about the bet. Here's an acronym I created to help put my story in perspective.

- B = Be disciplined in your career, in your life, and in your spiritual life. Hard work and perseverance are the keys here. Linking your passions to where you are heading is also key. Remember to start with small steps and grow through those steps to taking on more and more. The perseverance that being disciplined brings pays off every time.

- E = Execute your plan. First, you need a plan, and then you need the discipline to work it. And you will need to make midcourse corrections to reach your destination. Remember, it's not the destination but the journey that makes the difference. You must be the change.

> T = Take risks. Get out of your comfort zone. Challenge yourself to get better at your craft, whatever it is. Don't take reckless risks, but do take calculated risks. Understand as best as possible what all the risks are in whatever you are considering doing.

As I finish my seventh year as the CEO of Sharonview, I continue to look for ways to take our game and my leadership game to the next level. What new books, people, sermons, movies, music, podcasts, and so on will come my way that will allow me to improve? What existing relationships will be strengthened and deepened by challenging ourselves to work toward becoming the best version of ourselves?

Working harder on yourself than you do on your job and finding out what you are passionate about will take you places you never imagined. But make sure you have a written plan, and look back at where you have traveled over the last week, month, quarter, year, and years. It's important to stop and have those resting moments that allow you to take inventory of all you have accomplished thanks to your Nathans (your truth tellers), your Jonathans (lifelong friends on the journey with you) and your Samuels (your spiritual guides, wise counselors, mentors, and coaches).

Make the bet.

REFERENCES

Allen, D. 2001. *Getting Things Done: The Art of Stress Free Productivity.* New York: Penguin.

Batterson, M. 2017. *Whisper: How to Hear the Voice of God.* Colorado Springs: Crown Publishing.

Duckworth, A. 2016. *Grit: The Power of Passion and Perseverance.* New York: Scribner.

Hunter, J. C. 1998. *The Servant: A Simple Story about the True Essence of Leadership.* Rocklin, CA: Prima.

Lencioni, Patrick. 2016. *The Ideal Team Player: How to Recognize and Cultivate Three Essential Virtues; A Leadership Fable.* Hoboken, NJ: Jossey-Bass.

Maxwell, John C. 2011. *The Five Levels of Leadership: Proven Steps to Maximaize Your Potential.* New York: Center Street.

Maxwell, John C. 2014. *The Maxwell Leadership Bible.* Nashville, TN. Thomas Nelson.

Pink, D. 2009. *Drive: The Surprising Truth about What Motivates Us.* New York: Riverhead Books.

Reichheld, Fred. 2006. *The Ultimate Question.* Boston, MA. Harvard Business Review Press.

Rohn, J. 1996. *Seven Strategies for Wealth and Happiness: Power Ideas from America's Foremost Business Philosopher.* Rocklin, CA: Prima.

Wooden, John 2009. *Coach Wooden's Leadership Game Plan for Success: 12 Lessons for Extraordinary Performance and Personal Excellence.* New York: McGraw-Hill.

www.ingramcontent.com/pod-product-compliance
Lightning Source LLC
Chambersburg PA
CBHW021452210526
45463CB00002B/747